D1634032

Adventure
in Music

To Dorothy

By the same author

From a Music Lover's Armchair (1926)
The Appeal of Jazz (1927)
The Soul of Music (1950)
The Divine Quest in Music (1957)
Revelation in Shakespeare (1964)

THE AUTHOR

Adventure in Music

The Companion Volume to "The Soul of Music"

R. W. S. Mendl M.A. (OXON.)

Neville Spearman Limited
London, 1964

Printed and bound in Great Britain by The Garden City Press Limited, Letchworth, Hertfordshire for Neville Spearman Limited, 112 Whitfield Street, London, W.1

Contents

page

Preface 7

1. *Prologue:* the scope of this book 11

PART I : *Music and its creators*

2. What is a great composer? 15
3. The composer's "language" 26
4. The expressive power of music 36
5. Beethoven's second thoughts 48
6. Was Brahms a conservative? 51

PART II : *Interlude : Music and its audience*

7. Varieties of performance 59
8. Programmes 66

PART III : *Music, drama and dancing*

9. Reactions to ballet 71
10. Operatic symbolism 75
11. *Electra* in drama and music 85
12. Great tragic music-drama 90
13. Great operatic comedy 102
14. Shakespeare's influence on Berlioz 116
15. Mendelssohn and the problems of Shakespearean production 128
16. Verdi and Shakespeare 133
17. Shakespeare's *Henry VIII:* some musical analogies 137
18. Great love duets 140

page

PART IV : *How music can influence a poet*

19. Robert Browning, the poet-musician:
    (1) Biographical 151
20. Robert Browning, the poet-musician:
    (2) Music in Browning's poetry 162

PART V : *Conclusion*

21. Serenity 177
22. Epilogue 184

Index 187

Preface

My book *The Soul of Music* consisted of variations on the theme of the relationship between music and the world outside itself. In this volume I present a fresh set of variations on that theme. I have embodied in it, among other things, many of the ideas contained in articles contributed to *Musical Opinion, The Chesterian, Music and Letters,* and the Penguins *Music Magazine* and *Music;* I am grateful to their proprietors and editors for permission.

There are passages in some chapters which slightly overlap with one another: in a musical structure of this kind, though each variation is developed out of the main theme, usually each is an entity capable of being understood without reference to the others; similarly, while all my chapters are related to the main subject of the book, they can be read independently of one another, and so the occasional recurrence of the same thought, considered from divergent angles at relevant points in different chapters, is deliberate.

R. W. S. M.

Is it not strange that sheeps' guts should hale souls out of men's bodies?

Shakespeare: *Much Ado About Nothing*, II, iii

CHAPTER 1

Prologue: The Scope of this Book

IN MY BOOK *The Soul of Music* I sought to show how music, though the most independent of all the arts, is bound up with life at every turn. It can never exist in an ivory tower. Even the most abstract of sound patterns is analogous, as a (not very extensive) genre within the domain of music, to the pattern of a beautiful carpet in the visual sphere. Most music expresses emotions or religion or thoughts or characters (in generalized forms) or images in the external world. Those expressions can, it is true, only be conveyed in the musical forms in which they are in fact embodied, but they are nevertheless linked with their counterparts in the non-musical world.

Part I of this book relates to "music and its creators". This unique and independent medium of music has been utilized from time immemorial by all and sundry; but here I am chiefly concerned with its use by the great composers and with various ways in which their employment of it is associated with the external world. For this purpose, the first requirement is to try to clarify our minds on what we mean by "a great composer".

Now, the elements out of which composers have constructed their music in the past—their means of communication to listeners—have been described as "melody, rhythm, and harmony"—with "colour" acquiring greater importance since about 1800 than previously. But insufficient attention has been paid by writers on music to the importance of "themes", their difference from "melodies", and the place of "supreme melodies" as a factor in the greatness of a composer. The twelve-note system is a recent addition to the "language" of music which also calls for discussion.

These reflections lead naturally to a consideration of the expressive power of music, the manner in which it portrays character and the external world in general, the development of the resources by which it does so, and the problem of musical progress.

My next "variations" deal with Beethoven's second thoughts and the question whether Brahms was as "conservative" as has been thought hitherto.

An "Interlude" (Part II) raises the subjects of performance and of programmes, which are relevant to our theme, because they are concerned with the relationship of music to its audiences.

In Part III we return to the subject of the composer's actual creation and its connection with the external world. One of the spheres in that world with which it has been associated since the days of ancient Athenian drama is the theatre. Hence follow chapters dealing with reactions to ballet, operatic symbolism, *Electra* in drama and music, great tragic music-drama, great operatic comedy, and four aspects of the bond between Shakespeare and music; and a discussion of great love duets, which mostly occur in opera.

In Part IV I illustrate the influence of music on a poet, by taking the case of Robert Browning.

Lastly, it has seemed to me fitting to conclude with a chapter on serenity and its embodiment in the music of various great masters of the art, and finally an epilogue.

PART I

MUSIC AND ITS CREATORS

CHAPTER 2

What is a Great Composer?

I—Preliminary

THE QUESTION, WHO are the great composers, has frequently puzzled, fascinated, or irritated music lovers according to their temperament. Alfred Einstein devoted an interesting book to the subject of *Greatness in Music*, yet left us with no very clear idea of what he really meant by the words of its title. *The Times Literary Supplement* of 20th August 1954, reviewing Mr. Humphrey Searle's book *The Music of Liszt*, declared that Liszt, "like Berlioz, is not admitted into the ranks of the great composers but is awarded a status corresponding to '*proxime accessit*'." Yet it calls them both "highly original geniuses"; and if a composer is that and if his work continues to be enjoyed by countless music lovers for many generations, the question may well be asked, is he not great?

Both Berlioz and Liszt have long been controversial figures, but the elimination of Berlioz, at any rate, from the ranks of the great composers would restrict the field to an exceedingly narrow compass. Most of Liszt's choral works, and even some of his compositions in other spheres, have been put on the shelf for so long that they are virtually unknown to listeners today; and so, if survival is one of the tests of greatness, it might be argued, on this ground, that his is a borderline case. But most of Berlioz's works are performed from time to time, some of them frequently, to the delight of those who hear them. And those who love or appreciate his music would unhesitatingly call him a very great composer.

What, then, do we mean by "greatness" in music? Spiritual character, imagination, emotional range, descriptive power, a sense of form, technical mastery—all these are ingredients which we find in music that we call great. Not all of them, of course, occur in every "great" work: some and not others may be present in a composition; to a certain extent they may overlap; nor do I claim that my list is exhaustive.

II—Supreme Creators

Many of us, I imagine, find it attractive to try to decide who are the supreme creators in whatever field of art specially interests us. By "supreme" I do not mean merely "great", but those few giants who tower even over the other great ones by reason of their majesty and range, a universality of spirit, imagination and insight, and a width of transcendent humanity.

It is a fascinating quest, in which each of us has his own ideas, but which probably does produce some measure of agreement among lovers of art.

My own selection of poets would be Homer, Aeschylus, Sophocles, Vergil, Dante, Shakespeare, Milton, Goethe, Wordsworth and Browning. (To cover literature generally would be to open too wide a field.) If we consider painting, most people, I fancy, would include Giotto, Michelangelo, Raphael, Leonardo da Vinci, Botticelli, Titian, Rubens, Velasquez and Rembrandt —and maybe a few others; Pheidias and Michelangelo would clearly be numbered among the supreme sculptors, but I will not attempt to name others, for some of the finest sculpture in the world is anonymous. Many of the most beautiful buildings have been the work of a number of artists, whose identity in some cases is unknown; so let us leave architecture out of the discussion.

Now music, for reasons which I have tried to explain in chapters two and three of my book *The Soul of Music*, is the youngest of the arts in the sense (only) that the names of those whom music-lovers today would call truly great did not begin to appear until the fifteenth century: the absence of notation for the music of antiquity; its perpetual unison, which we should find wearisome; its lack of "colour"; the slowness in the development of instruments, which required science that was beyond the range of ancient peoples; and perhaps above all, the independence of music, as contrasted with the reference which the other arts have to the external world and which made them better adapted for early civilizations than music could be. Nevertheless, there are eight composers whom I feel bound to include in my short list of supreme creators and whose creative work was spread over no more than two hundred years —Bach and Handel, Haydn and Mozart, Beethoven and Schubert, Wagner and Brahms; and of those I, in common with many people, place Beethoven and Bach above all the rest. In them, all the ingredients of greatness seem to be combined in the highest degree, though some music lovers find the supreme union of these great qualities in one of them more than in the other.

Bach was the greatest of all composers of sacred music for voices, and of music for organ, for solo violin and solo 'cello. Beethoven was the supreme creator of all other forms of instrumental music, and his *Missa Solennis* alone equals Bach's B minor setting of the Mass. Bach's greatest music, whilst absolutely amazing in its technical skill, is either profoundly religious, vividly pictorial and descriptive, or directly expressive of vivid moods and feelings; even his dance movements have a spiritual grace. Beethoven's art is imbued with a spiritual quality which is to be found even in the compositions of his early period, deepens in the works of his maturity, and rises to infinite mystery in his third period with its crowning glories. If there is a meaning in sublimity,[1] there are more instances of sublime music in Bach and Beethoven than in any other composers hitherto.

I have a special term for those whom I regard as the supreme creative artists. I think of them as "glory men". Beethoven regarded Handel as the greatest of his predecessors; but much of the finest music of Bach was inevitably unknown to him, and eminent composers are not always good critics. Handel was, however, unquestionably a "glory man", with his majestic choruses and the grace or sweetness or splendid vigour of his arias and instrumental movements. Does the term fit Haydn and Mozart? Not so far as the earlier works of Mozart in his "galant" style are concerned; but his greatest music—for

[1] I have discussed the meaning of sublimity in *The Divine Quest in Music*, pp. 232–5.

instance, the "Linz", the "Prague", and the last three symphonies, so many of his pianoforte concertos, the quartets dedicated to Haydn, the clarinet quintet, the string quintets in C and G minor (K.515–16), parts of the Mass in C minor—is "glorious", not merely "beautiful". The music of *Figaro* transcends its subject. There is tragic grandeur in *Idomeneo* and in the music that precedes the downfall of Don Giovanni in an opera called a "dramma giocoso". *The Magic Flute* is a blend of childlike wonderland and spiritual glory. Mozart was "myriad-minded", even though he was not so tremendous as Shakespeare.

Haydn dedicated his great genius to God throughout his long life, and the range of moods in his vast output of symphonies and string quartets is prodigious. He poured out his soul to the Lord not only in the wonders and sweetness of *The Creation* and in the sublimity of *The Seven Words of Our Saviour on the Cross*, but also in *The Seasons* with its fragrance and its simple fidelity to Nature.

I regard Schubert as the greatest of all song writers; even though Wolf wedded music to words more closely, Schubert had a more wondrous lyrical gift, and was also the creator of two of the supreme symphonies of the world, and of some of the most beautiful chamber music and works for pianoforte. A genius so inspired, so many-sided, qualifies him for inclusion among the "glory men".

Some deny the presence of a spiritual quality in the art of Wagner—a charge, which, if true, would certainly reduce his stature; but they overlook the nobility inherent in so much of his music and the fact that as a musical dramatist it was his *métier* to get inside the skins of his characters and to present evil in contrast to good, as Shakespeare did. Berlioz had a somewhat smaller emotional range, and his sense of form was not so consummate, but in the other characteristics which I have mentioned he was almost Wagner's equal—perhaps fully equal to him in spiritual quality when we remember *L'Enfance du Christ*, the *Messe des Morts*, and the *Te Deum*. It has been said that Wagner's art is voluptuous, and that its religion is false. But it is voluptuous only when dramatic antithesis requires this, as with the Venusberg and the Flower Maidens. The love-death music of *Tristan* is intense, not voluptuous, and takes on a mystical cast; and Wagner's handling of the legend reveals nobility.[2] The vast range of *The Ring* shows an "infinite variety" of the forces of humanity and nature and a supernatural world, and reaches a majestic culmination. *Die Meistersinger* is a golden tale of love and friendship. *Parsifal* is imbued with a celestial mysticism. Wagner was a Titan, only surpassed by Bach and Beethoven because they reached even greater heights of sublimity and purity of vision.

Outside the realms of opera, Brahms was the greatest composer of the second half of the nineteenth century, very largely because of the majestic quality of his art. The *German Requiem* is the supreme achievement in sacred choral music since Beethoven, and when we contemplate the grandeur of his four symphonies and of the *Tragic Overture*, the two tremendous piano concertos, the rich humanity of the violin concerto and of the one for violin and 'cello, the varied wonders of his concerted chamber music and of his works for solo pianoforte, and the loveliness of his songs—even though he lacked Wolf's instinct for poetry—we find in him a profundity and an emotional range which exalt his genius to a supreme pinnacle.

III—Other Great Composers

My eight supreme composers were all Germans or Austrians. This does not signify that I have any predilection for a Teutonic outlook in music, if indeed there is such a thing. It simply means that the few composers whom I regard as intrinsically greater than all others were in fact Teutons. My supreme "glory men" in the other arts came from various countries. But the question whether it is purely fortuitous that in music, hitherto, they have all been of Teutonic stock, gives rise to deeper problems.

We have seen that the truly great composers did not begin to appear until the fifteenth century; whereas the great names in the other arts have been spread over far longer periods, although those arts are not themselves of greater antiquity

[2] For a fuller discussion of this subject, I would refer the reader to my books *The Soul of Music* (p. 238) and *The Divine Quest in Music* (pp. 217–18).

than music. May not this fact have a bearing on the Teutonic monopoly of the supreme musical composers in the course of two hundred years? Poetry, painting and sculpture all came to maturity so long before music that there has been time for great successions of gigantic geniuses to appear in one nation and then in another, and so it is that, for instance, the world has been enriched in turn by the wondrous poetry and sculpture of ancient Greece, the great painting of Renaissance Italy and of seventeenth century Holland, the masterpieces of the Italian Dante at the end of the Middle Ages and of the English poets in the fourteenth, sixteenth, seventeenth and nineteenth centuries especially.

The eight musical "glory men" from Germany and Austria all belonged to the eighteenth and nineteenth centuries; in the course of the five hundred years of what I may term the full fruition of the art, there has, perhaps, not been sufficient time for another epoch of equal grandeur. But most of the great composers of the next rank have come from other nations—some of them earlier in date than Bach and Handel, others contemporaneous with the eight or just subsequent to them.

From England came Dunstable, Tallis, Byrd, Dowland, Morley, Weelkes, Wilbye and Orlando Gibbons—to name no more among the Tudor and Jacobean masters; Purcell in the seventeenth century; Sullivan (as a great creator of light music), Elgar (the greatest of all composers since Brahms, in my view), Delius, Holst, Vaughan Williams, Walton, and Britten, in the nineteenth and twentieth centuries; and posterity may decide to include others now living in our midst. From Italy arose Palestrina and Monteverdi in the age before Bach and Handel; the two Scarlattis; Rossini and Verdi in the nineteenth century; and in France from the fifteenth to the twentieth centuries Josquin des Prés, Couperin le Grand, Rameau, Berlioz, Franck (whom we may perhaps regard as "shared" by her with Belgium), Bizet, Debussy and Fauré; and from the Netherlands, Dufay and Lassus in the fifteenth and sixteenth centuries. From Russia, a succession of eminent composers began in the nineteenth century, of whom anyhow Mussorgsky and Tchaikovsky must be called "great". Spain gave us Vittoria in the sixteenth century and Falla in our own times, even if Albeniz and Granados are considered minor masters. The Czechs produced Smetana, Dvořák and Janáček. Poland, Denmark and Finland have each given birth to one great genius in Chopin, Nielsen and Sibelius. Switzerland produced Ernest Bloch—a great modern Jewish composer who ultimately became a citizen of the U.S.A.

Thus from many other nations in those five hundred years have arisen at one time or another musical creators great enough to be matched against Teutonic masters other than the eight supreme ones—that is to say, against Schütz, Gluck and Weber, Mendelssohn and Schumann, Bruckner and Wolf, certainly against Mahler and Richard Strauss. I do not, of course, suggest anything approaching equality among these great artists of various nations who are beneath the very topmost level; nor do I wish to deny the term "greatness" to some whom I have not named, but whom I would place below them.

Germany and Austria (as I pointed out in *The Soul of Music*, chapter nineteen) began to lose their unrivalled hegemony after Beethoven and Schubert, and in the twentieth century hitherto Teutonic music has not risen to greater heights than that of certain other nations. It is quite feasible that, as time goes on, other supreme creators, comparable with some at least of the mighty eight, may arise, and no one can foretell from which nations they may come. The Teutonic lands have had their golden age of musical supremacy, even as great Italian painting ran its course for a few hundred years and the glory of Dutch pictorial art blossomed in the course of a century.

IV—On the Borderline

The reason why the great masters mentioned above can be grouped in a category second only to that of the eight "glory men" is, I suggest, simply that their art contains all or some of the ingredients of "greatness" outlined earlier in this chapter[3], in a more intense degree than other composers such as, for example, Cherubini, Lulli, Donizetti, Bellini, Borodin, Rimsky-Korsakov, Grieg, Puccini, or Ravel, who are, in effect, minor masters—"great" creators only by the skin of their teeth, as it were, or even borderline cases. But a composer may also, in our judgment, fail to qualify for inclusion in that second category because of an element of flamboyance or even falseness in his artistic make-up. The two most striking examples of this that occur to me are Liszt and Richard Strauss. Both are "great", but only just!

Sometimes in Liszt there is a touch of bombast, and often his music is excessively ornate: this does not mean, however, that its emotion is not genuine, but simply that his art, though sincere, is the product of a very ornate personality: when we compare his piano music with that of Chopin, we find that many of his trappings are merely elaborate tinsel, whereas Chopin's are integral poetic elements in the beautiful fabric—or, to borrow a different simile, as fresh and fragrant as the foliage of a tree.

Strauss is a different case. He possessed many of the qualities of a great composer. He was a brilliant master of the orchestra, and had a sense of structure which enabled him to apply such forms as a rondo and a theme and variations even to symphonic poems like *Till Eulenspiegel* and *Don Quixote*, and to turn the "leitmotiv" system to good account in his operas. He was a skilful, though often superficial, painter of musical portraits. He certainly had descriptive power and imagination. Yet his art is too often hollow, and superficially "entrancing" by reason of a surface charm exhibited with juicy orchestration that only serves to conceal the rottenness beneath—if, indeed, it does conceal it. He could not express transfiguration convincingly, because, for all his gifts in conveying morbid and psychopathic subtleties, he was not a big enough artist to be able to do so, with the result that the closing section of *Tod und Verklärung* is tawdry and cheap. The "hero" in *Ein Heldenleben* turns out to be none other than Strauss himself, the "enemies" being merely adverse critics of his music and "the hero's works of peace" consisting of excerpts from other compositions of his. The merits of the *Sinfonia Domestica* and the *Alpine Symphony* lie mostly in their brilliant orchestration. *Der Rosenkavalier* is the embodiment of superficial sophistication, tricked out in luscious orchestral colour, but lacking in

[a] See Section I (above).

genuine emotion and in that *real* charm which cannot exist without sincerity. A handful of Strauss's songs is in the straight succession of true poetical music handed down by the greater *lieder* composers, Schubert and Schumann, Brahms and Wolf. There is authenticity in his symphonic poems *Macbeth, Till Eulenspiegel, Don Juan*, and *Don Quixote. Metamorphosen* and the Recognition scene in *Elektra* show what he could do in the way of genuine pathos and nobility. But elsewhere there is too much "fake" in his musical expression of emotion to qualify him for anything above the lowest class among the great ones—immeasurably below his contemporaries, Elgar, Carl Nielsen, and Sibelius, who are constantly authentic artists and, moreover, equal him, where they do not surpass him, in the other elements of greatness. I have written elsewhere[4] more fully about Elgar and Sibelius; it is sufficient here to say that Elgar's music is either profoundly religious or steadfastly related to the true emotions or aspirations of men, women and children; and that Sibelius is a genuine poet of humanity, myth, and Nature. Nielsen, who was not, in the normal sense, religious, was deeply concerned to reveal in his art the conflicts and victories of human existence, and succeeded triumphantly in doing so.

V—Greatness in Miniature

It has been said[5] that, though it may take great art (in the sense of the presence in high degree of both skill and imagination) to make a miniature, nevertheless a miniature is not a great work of art, however beautiful, though its beauty has nothing whatever to do with its size.

There seems to be a certain confusion of thought here. If skill and imagination and beauty, in high degree, are all present, I suggest that the result is a great work of art. Size, in the sense of length in the case of music or drama, is irrelevant. Sibelius's Seventh Symphony is one of the greatest symphonies of modern times, though it takes only twenty minutes to perform and is

[4] In *The Soul of Music* and *The Divine Quest in Music, passim.*
[5] In an article in *The Times* of 7th October 1949.

thus shorter than any since the early ones of Haydn and Mozart; true, it is in one movement, but this contains, as it were in a compressed form, many of the ingredients which in other symphonies are spread over several movements. Its greatness consists in its grandeur and beauty and skill. Longer symphonies than any of Beethoven's first eight, such as some of Mahler's, may be beautiful, or show greatness in some portions, but are felt to be less great than his, partly because they sprawl or the composer is unable to sustain the inspiration or his creative faculty at a sufficiently high level throughout the work. No one, however, would call Sibelius's Seventh a "miniature symphony", for all its brevity.

Bigness of conception in a work would presumably prevent anyone from applying the word "miniature" to it. Aristotle in the *Poetics* says that the action of tragedy must be serious, complete, and possessing size: the size to which he refers does seem to mean length, but then he was speaking of tragic drama, and it is his word which we translate "serious" that is more related to the greatness which we are now considering.

There is no reason why the briefest of works should not be great. Many of the short lyrics of Wordsworth, Keats and Shelley and of the sonnets of Shakespeare and Donne, for instance, merit the title. Chopin only excelled as a composer for the piano, and mostly of short pieces; but sometimes they are intrinsically tremendous like the Étude in A minor (op. 25, no. 11), the Nocturne in G (op. 37, no. 2), the Preludes in D flat and A flat (op. 28, nos. 15 and 17), and even when they are slighter they are great works of art. The Prelude in C minor (op. 28, no. 20) is grand and tragic in its content, as well as highly skilled and imaginative, and therefore qualifies for being a great work of art, brief though it is. The question remains whether it is a miniature, and the answer to be given would affect many of the most deeply felt songs of Schubert and others. Chopin has usually been considered to be an exquisite creator of miniatures (though not necessarily only of those), and therefore, we have to make up our minds what we mean by a miniature. If the C minor Prelude is one, then miniatures certainly can be great works of art; even if it is not, but if many of the same composer's waltzes and mazurkas and the two Études in

G flat (op. 10, no. 5, and op. 25, no. 9) are rightly called miniatures, are these on that account to be debarred from being "great works of art"?

Wolf composed many exquisite miniatures, but also such songs as the stupendous "Prometheus" and the majestic "Grenzen der Menschheit"; and he is great even when he is not speaking of big things, just as Brahms, the giant who created the *German Requiem* and the supreme instrumental music of the second half of the nineteenth century, was also great when he was composing waltzes whether for piano solo or for solo voices and piano duet.

"Miniature" denotes a work on a small scale, but it also implies that its maker, in creating it, was not concerned with the great issues of life and death and religion or even with the most profound emotions. That does not in itself prevent the composition from being great. Light music may be great, if it possesses loveliness, skill and imagination. Byrd, Handel, Bach, Gluck, Haydn, Mozart, even Beethoven at times, Schubert, Chopin, Mendelssohn, Brahms, Tchaikovsky and Elgar, have all been composers of light art as well as serious. Many of Sullivan's lyrics and dances in the Savoy operas are great music, though light. At its best, his work has imagination, a certain range of emotion, a sense of form, a consummate gift for dainty orchestration, and a fragrance particularly appropriate to the art of comic opera; and it continues to give delight three quarters of a century after it was written. Sullivan did not write any great music that was not light. His serious works were not great. Johann Strauss the younger did not compose serious music of any account; he is often called a great composer of waltzes: this is the same thing as saying that his waltzes—or some of them—are great, and whether we think them so or not is a matter for our judgment in each case. There is no reason why a waltz, just because it belongs to the domain of light music, should not be a great work of art.

VI—To wind up

We could hardly call a composer great, if, for example, he

wrote only one great song or minuet. But if his work reveals some of the qualities to which I have referred, in sufficient measure to result in its maintaining its appeal to successive generations, that is evidence in favour of his greatness. The outcome will, no doubt, be a much longer list than those who would exclude even Berlioz would have us think; but unless we are to confine the term "great composers" to a mere handful who can be numbered in single figures, I believe this to be a truer account.

CHAPTER 3

The Composer's "Language"[1]

I—Its basic elements

THE BASIC ELEMENTS of the "language" of music—the means by which its composers convey emotions, thoughts, and aspirations to listeners—have often been said to be "melody", "rhythm", and "harmony", although melody and rhythm obviously overlap: a melody must have rhythm, though rhythm can exist independently. Rhythm was an intuitive result of the pulse and the heart-beat. Melody (or "tune") arose from the cries of primitive man in proclaiming his needs or accompanying the steps of his dances. Harmony—in our sense

[1] Suzanne K. Langer is doubtless, strictly speaking, right when she says (in *Feeling and Form*, pp. 29, 31) that "music is not a language . . . because its elements are not words—independent associative symbols with a reference fixed by convention". In speaking of it as a "language" in this book I am, of course, using the word in a broad sense, to indicate that music is a medium which can convey, in its own idiom, emotions, thoughts, characters and even to some extent events and scenes of the external world. Since writing most of this book I have read Deryck Cooke's *The Language of Music* (Oxford University Press, 1959), and am glad to find that his thorough researches into the philosophy and technique of this subject have brought him—most convincingly—to the same broad conclusion as I have reached independently regarding music as a means of expressing emotion, etc.

of notes of different pitch simultaneously sounded (as opposed to the ancient Greek "harmonia", which was a fitting together of notes in sequence, more like our melodic line)—apparently only came into existence in medieval times, and has been the subject of countless treatises and textbooks. And once it was firmly established, melodies could no longer be heard without the subconscious assumption of harmonies beneath them. Musical "colour", a fourth element, though it dates from the beginnings of the art, became far more important from Berlioz onwards.[2] Melody, as a subject, tends rather to be taken for granted by music lovers; we all know—or think we know—what we mean by "a good tune".

Obviously, it is the use which the composer makes of all these elements that constitutes the chief value of a composition as a whole; but the importance of pregnant, significant, or beautiful themes or melodies in themselves has been liable to be underrated in modern musical thinking. In this chapter I shall consider the difference between themes and melodies, their place in the art of music, the relationship of "supreme melodies" to the great composers, and conclude with some thoughts about the new musical language known as the twelve-note system.

II—Themes and Melodies

There have been various ideas about the terms "theme" and "melody": that they are synonymous; that they represent two species of a class to which no satisfactory name can be given; that a theme is a sort of melody, or even that it is simply a short melody; that whilst there is no distinction in kind between the two things, "theme" is the more comprehensive expression, and that a melody is just a special sort of theme.

In my view, a theme differs from a melody in somewhat the same way as a phrase differs from a complete sentence: a melody must have an appreciable length, and the rise or fall of its curve usually leads to some sort of conclusion or cadence; a

[2] I dealt with "The Value of Colour" in chapter fourteen of *The Soul of Music*.

so-called "theme" on which variations are made, may be really a melody. Some very simple compositions, such as folk-songs, may consist of little else than one melody, with or without harmony.

In a symphonic or contrapuntal movement, a theme or melody is a talking-point from which the body of the music is developed. The movement is evolved out of these principal subjects, which are transformed, varied, combined, repeated. It has been said that their quality plays little or no part in the value of the composition as a whole—the manner of using them being the only precious thing. In support of this belief, it is pointed out that, for instance, Beethoven occasionally employed other people's thematic or melodic ideas, that Handel perhaps borrowed more in that way than any other composer, and that a great piece of music may be constructed from weak materials. This is a strange conception. It has been suggested that the principal subject of the great opening Allegro of the "Eroica" is not of special moment; true, it is largely framed in the notes of the tonic chord, but this in itself proves nothing, except that the melody is free from complication. The value of it lies in its strong, buoyant rhythm, and in the fitting of the accents to the tones precisely in the manner which seems appropriate to the firmness of the outlines. The beginning of the Finale—a flourish, and then the bass of the future melody played *pizzicato* softly on the strings—is almost insignificant, and even the charming melody which follows is itself scarcely heroic; but I believe this to be deliberate—a symbol that a great leader or benefactor of men may start from undistinguished beginnings.[3] The opening subject of Beethoven's C minor Symphony has been called unremarkable in itself—three short G's followed by a long E flat; yet its first announcement is most striking, even after repeated hearings of the work; moreover, as Tovey pointed out,[4] these are really only the first four notes of the whole big theme, which lasts for twenty-one bars.

Those who believe in the unimportance of themes or melodies in an extended movement are perhaps misled by the fact that some of the most pregnant ones in music are remarkably

[3] This idea is discussed more fully in *The Divine Quest in Music*, pp. 82–3.
[4] *Essays in Musical Analysis*, vol. I, p. 40.

simple: they mistake simplicity for insignificance. If we try to find an inspired movement in the works of the great composers, made out of poor or trivial subjects, we shall find it a hard task. The chief reason why the gay Finale of Beethoven's B flat Trio (op. 97) is not up to the level of the three magnificent preceding movements is that it is based on a less striking theme and never fully recovers from this disadvantage.

This does not imply that the full significance or potentialities of a subject can be appreciated from the first statement of it. No one, hearing the opening themes (or melodies) of the "Eroica" or C minor Symphonies for the first time could possibly dream of the wondrous fabric which was woven from them. Nobody could tell in advance the delightful story that Bach is going to unfold from the determined subject with which he begins his D major fugue in the First Book of the "Forty-eight", or guess what Mozart will do with the wistful melody which opens his G minor Symphony (K. no. 550). Brahms alone could have seen the possibilities in the charming *St. Antony Chorale.* But to say that the quality of the subject is, in each case, unimportant, is quite another matter. A great building cannot be erected on insecure foundations.

III—Supreme Melodies

Most of the greatest melodies in the world have been created by the greatest composers and form the basis of extended movements; and incidentally, the idea that themes, rather than melodies, should be the material for movements in sonata form is to some extent discounted by this fact; in quick movements themes may generally be more frequent, because they are more suitable than melodies; but in slow movements the *tempo* allows the spaciousness of a complete melody to unfold itself.

Let us consider some instances.

Bach, the king of counterpoint, the brilliant craftsman, was also the inventor of some of the supreme melodies. It is natural, in so great a master of vocal music, that some of these should be airs for solo voices—the cantatas are full of them—but the deeply religious Aria in the Third Orchestral Suite and the solemn Adagio from the Second Violin Concerto are outstanding examples for instruments. And he composed some of his greatest melodies as what would often be called instrumental "accompaniments" to the vocal line, and as sacred as that in character—like the organ part in the chorale *Jesu, Joy of Man's Desiring* or the violin solo in the aria "Have Mercy" from the *St. Matthew Passion.*

Beethoven, the supreme architect of sonata form, the master who excelled at weaving great masterpieces from short, pregnant themes, was also the composer of many of the world's most glorious melodies. To name only a few, think of the noble grief of the great air in F minor which opens the Adagio in the First Razoumovsky Quartet (op. 59, no. 1); the serene beauty of the D major melody in the Andante of the B flat Trio (op. 97); the mystical loveliness of the tune of the slow movement in the E major Sonata (op. 109); the solo violin part, descending, as it were, from heaven to earth, in the Benedictus of the *Missa Solennis;* the celestial vision of the main subject in the Adagio of the Ninth Symphony, and the great melody of Joy in the Finale; and lastly, the equally simple, unutterably peaceful, sublimity of the melody of the Lento in his final Quartet (op. 135), which inspired Brahms in the creation of the glorious second subject in the slow movement of his Fourth Symphony; there is a rhythmic resemblance, and in both of them a prevalence of consecutive notes of the scale, in the one case descending and ascending, in the other the reverse.

Handel was not only the welder of majestic choruses and a charming miniaturist, but also one of the world's great melody writers. "He shall feed his flock", "Ombra mai fu" (the famous "Largo"), and "Silent Worship" (from *Ptolemy*) are only a few of the supremely beautiful airs to be found in his vast output. The feeling in the music needs no verbal description here—it is an expression, or an idealization, of the spirit of the words.

Music flowed out of Haydn, Mozart and Schubert,[5] and the

[5] Maurice J. E. Brown, in his book *Schubert, a critical biography,* has shown how carefully that composer sketched and prepared his work before completing it: Schubert's art was not so "effortless" as used to be believed; nevertheless, composition did not cost either Haydn or Mozart or him such labour and toil as it did, e.g., Beethoven. These things are largely a matter of degree.

astonishing thing is that such apparently spontaneous art should have produced both consummate workmanship and heavenly melodies. Think only of the perfect happiness of the opening tune of the first Allegro in Haydn's Symphony No. 104 in D, or the beautiful dream which pervades the Adagio in his String Quartet op. 77, no. 1; the serene second subject of the first movement in Mozart's String Quartet in D minor (K.421), or the melody that begins "Voi che sapete" in *Figaro,* where Mozart portrays romantic love in music that transcends both the personality of Cherubino and the immediate situation in which it occurs; the tranquil devotion of Schubert's "Du bist die Ruh' ", or the wondrous peace that reigns in the second subject of the opening movement of his great Quintet for Strings in C (op. 163).

With Wagner and Verdi we venture on more controversial ground. Verdi was, I feel, a great composer of melodies, rather than a composer of superbly great melodies. Of course there are lovely melodies in his early and middle-period operas, but I personally would hesitate to call them "supreme". Verdi was at his greatest in *Otello* and *Falstaff,* but by the time he came to write these he had passed from composing the formal, rounded, arias of his earlier days, in favour of a more continuous flow of sound, constructed from themes rather than tunes. His other greatest works—the *Requiem* and the *Quattro Pezzi Sacri*—are notable for qualities other than outstanding greatness of melody.

Wagner wrote melodies galore in his early operas, many of them beautiful, all of them appropriate; but the supreme Wagner is to be found in *The Ring, Tristan, Meistersinger* and *Parsifal,* and in these he had taken to "unending melody", and for the most part had given up composing distinct melodies: their motives are pregnant themes, which undergo constant transformations but are not complete "sentences"; the "Spring Song" in the *Walküre* and the "Preislied" in the *Meistersinger* are exceptional instances of separable, lyrical songs, and even they, for all their beauty, are not, I venture to think, supreme among the purple patches of Wagner's glorious art.

Brahms combined mastery of structure with melodic supremacy: the fact that the triumphant main tune in the Finale of his First Symphony was indebted to Beethoven's "Joy" melody does not prevent it from being magnificent in its own right; the sublime melody on the 'cello that opens the Andante of the Second Pianoforte Concerto represents Brahms at the height of his powers; the "lullaby" of the Intermezzo for pianoforte in E flat (op. 117, no. 1) is at once noble and serene.

The examples which I have taken are all from seven out of my eight supreme composers—Wagner being the eighth. Of course, some of the world's greatest melodies are to be found elsewhere too: Gluck's "Che faro" and "O malheureuse Iphigénie", in both of which he uses the major key for an expression of exalted grief; the melody of idyllic love which enters on the horns and 'cellos in the "Scène d'Amour" in Berlioz's *Roméo et Juliette,* and the tranquil, fragrant piety of the "March of the Pilgrims" in his *Harold in Italy;* the calm beauty of the opening refrain in Chopin's Étude in E (op. 10, no. 3) and the peaceful loveliness of the second subject in the slow movement of his F minor pianoforte concerto (op. 21); the majestic "Nimrod" melody in Elgar's *Enigma Variations,* and the regret, dignity, and exaltation embodied in the tune of the Adagio in his 'cello concerto. These are a few samples which occur to me, though other music lovers would doubtless have their own ideas on the subject.

Familiarity has a good deal to do with the recognition of melodic beauty, and it may be too soon to decide whether to include any twentieth century instances apart from Elgar; but I wonder whether others will feel disposed to add any melodies in the twelve-note technique!

A composer may shine, as Tchaikovsky did, in the creation of lovely melodies and in the loveliness of his instrumentation of them, yet show a certain weakness in their development; but even the greatest composers (who excel as musical architects whether on a large or a small scale), in so far as they invented melodies rather than themes, owe part of their stature to a supreme beauty of melody.

And it is significant that whatever melodies—or themes—we may consider to be supreme or even simply "great" are always expressions of emotions, thoughts or aspirations which have their counterparts in the world outside music, and are not mere sound patterns.

IV—The New Languages

It remains to say something about the new languages, and particularly about the twelve-note music, the strange technique evolved by Schönberg when he turned his back on the melodic and harmonic system on which he had been brought up. Although it appeared early in this century, it is still "new": for it made a break with the past, very many music lovers have not yet become accustomed to it, and it has not hitherto died an early death, but has on the contrary been taken up by a number of subsequent composers in various countries.

Schönberg conceived the idea because he felt that, so far as he was concerned, the major-minor system which had prevailed for over two centuries had played itself out. He had written in it himself, in such works as the string sextet *Verklärte Nacht*, the D minor quartet (op. 7), and the choral and orchestral *Gurrelieder*. The chromaticism of the sixteenth century Italian madrigalists and still more of J. S. Bach, who in the eighteenth century anticipated so many future developments, had already been stretched almost to the furthest limits compatible with tonality by Wagner in *Tristan* and *Parsifal*, and Debussy had started to build chords on the interval of the fourth instead of the third. Schönberg decided to give chromaticism complete freedom. "Away with 'keys' ", was, in effect, his cry; "let us abolish the tonic, the dominant, and the sub-dominant; and, as there are twelve notes in the chromatic scale, let us build music on a basis of four twelve-note tone-rows; you can transpose each of these rows to the twelve notes of that scale, and thus have forty-seven variations of the first row, giving yourself plenty of scope for invention. There's no need for anyone who wants to go on with the old major-minor business to follow my example; but, for my part, I've done with it!" Splendid! But there was one big snag: chromaticism had been chiefly a melodic affair, a matter of successive notes: it was horizontal; it functioned by means of "accidentals"—moving from one note to another that was foreign to the key in which the piece, or the passage, was written; and therefore the new twelve-note system is also horizontal, and its technique is contrapuntal, not harmonic. For all that its practitioners care, the effect of the resulting *simultaneous* sounds on the listener is irrelevant. No wonder that so many music lovers, even among those belonging to the younger generation, find it distressing to the ear, though it is theoretically and intellectually fascinating and very interesting to the eye, for those who rejoice in working out puzzles on paper.

The earlier changes and developments in the language of music were evolutionary. The major and minor scales were simply two survivors of the eight ecclesiastical modes, the other six having gradually fallen out of favour; and the chromaticism has an ancient history, reaching its culmination in the nineteenth century. But to abolish keys altogether and to substitute tone-rows for them, was a wholly arbitrary and far more sudden, change, even though we can trace the steps that led to it. And we find that in practice twelve-note music appeals mainly to a small minority of devoted adherents. Schönberg's own compositions in this medium have tended to be outshone by those of Alban Berg, whom Sibelius wittily described as "Schönberg's best work"; and it is significant that Berg's famous opera *Wozzeck* does not wholly follow the system and that the passages which grip the ordinary music lover most are just those in which the composer reverts to the old tonality—Marie's prayer and the moving, though still dissonant, orchestral interlude before the last scene. Again, Berg's violin concerto, though mainly in the twelve-note idiom, contains various elements of tonal music, especially in its serene ending.

Bartók was also anxious to rid himself of "the tyranny of the Western major and minor modes", as he expressed it. But he was not a twelve-note man, except to a small extent; he reverted to various antique scales, Oriental, pentatonic and modal, made use of the whole tone scale and quarter tones, and sometimes treated chromatic intervals as independent degrees of the scale *à la* Schönberg; his methods were very flexible, and in his later works, such as the violin concerto, the concerto for orchestra, and the third piano concerto, his art became increasingly approachable to the ordinary music lover as it returned more closely to tonality, whilst still retaining its individual character.

One of the most revolutionary modern composers, Messiaen, has different ideas again about a musical language. Melody, he says (in his *Technique de mon langage musical*), should be the chief element, to which rhythm and harmony must be subservient; and the old rules of harmony and form are not to be rejected, but to be observed, expanded or increased by the addition of still older ones (derived from the Hindus or from plainsong) or more recent ones based on Debussy and all contemporary music. He likes specially the augmented fourth and the major sixth. And his musical aims are religious and mystical. Be that as it may, his mature compositions are exceedingly hard on the ear of the ordinary listener; but at any rate he is not tied to the wheel of the twelve-note system.

It is not necessary for music to be consistently beautiful in order to possess merit or to be great[6]: sometimes harshness may be required, to correspond to the words, situations or emotions of the song or the libretto; or the music may need to be cunningly descriptive in a sense which precludes actual beauty; but if it is to survive, listeners must be able to say that in the widest sense of the term they find the work enjoyable; and the difficulty which most music lovers find with the twelve-note compositions of Schönberg, von Webern, and others, is that even with the most open-minded approach they cannot get enjoyment from them. They may be interested to make their acquaintance, they may admire the composer's ingenuity, and respect his enterprise and industry, but they cannot overcome the obstacle that here is an avowedly fresh language of music which continues to grate upon their ears even with repeated hearings; that the work of its practitioners appeals to them precisely in so far as it occasionally leaves the shackles of twelve-note technique behind and reverts to the language of keys which it has tried, unsuccessfully, to displace; and that the alleged "tyranny" of the major and minor scales is really far more liberal and flexible. Many striking modern composers whose music, with its individual and original character, appeals to their contemporaries—Walton, Hindemith, Shostakovich, Britten and others—have held aloof from this particular method, Stravinsky has only taken to it in his old age, and many

[6] This subject is discussed more fully in *The Soul of Music*, pp. 226–8.

musicians and music lovers feel that it represents a theory which somehow does not work out satisfactorily in practice. They may, of course, still prove to be wrong; time alone will show; but meanwhile the twelve-note system is already far advanced into middle age. Those of us who do not react to it sympathetically must be pardoned if we suspect that it is too self-conscious, too theoretical, too arbitrary and artificial a change to be permanently and generally adopted, though it may continue to be used to a small extent in conjunction with other idioms; and that music is more likely to develop by a natural process of evolution; there are infinite possibilities for an enlargement of its scope, in the technical field, by harmonic and contrapuntal permutations and combinations, by melodic invention, by rhythmic variety, by experiments in colour, yet all within the wide ambit of key relationships which form the background of our musical consciousness.

Boulez, Stockhausen, the purveyors of *musique concrète* and the "extemporizers", have ventured even further into the abyss than Schönberg, Von Webern, or Messiaen have done. A minority of lovers of the art like this music, or profess to like it. Some even of the critics, perhaps afraid to be "out of date", behave like the woman in Ionesco's play who didn't really want to turn into a rhinoceros but pleaded that "one must move with the times". What nonsense it all is! let us remember Hans Andersen's story of *The Emperor's New Clothes*.

CHAPTER 4

The Expressive Power of Music

THE GREAT COMPOSERS of the past have not, as a rule, either by word or deed, indicated that they considered the main function of their art to be to create patterns in sound. When Stravinsky and others purported at one stage to put not merely romance but even emotion behind them, it was customary for their followers to cite Mozart as their great prototype, and to claim the virginal pieces of the Tudor masters as precedents for abstract instrumental art. Yet Mozart himself aspired always to opera. I do not suggest that he was right in his diagnosis of his own capabilities: for me, the greatest of his symphonies, the wonderful chain of pianoforte concertos, the finest of his chamber music, at least a handful of his works for piano solo, and certain parts of the Mass in C minor, are equal to any of his operas; but the fact that he regarded opera as the ideal art-form so far as the voicing of his own gifts was concerned, shows that he certainly did not view music as being primarily a matter of beautiful abstract designs, especially as opera at his hands was, in its own very different way, just as much "music drama" as Wagner's art was subsequently to be. Hadow[1] regarded the chief merit of Mozart's operas as being a succession of lovely numbers like "La ci darem", "Batti, Batti", "Voi che sapete", and so on; E. J. Dent[2] showed how the composer portrayed and developed human character and transmuted the story into terms of music. Mozart might introduce airs to suit the wishes of individual singers, but they were expressions of feeling, not just displays of virtuosity. If he wrote coloratura for the Queen of the Night, it was coloratura with a difference, portraying anger or agitation; its devices are exceedingly difficult to sing, but they are as integral to the character of the Queen and to the dramatic situation as Chopin's embroideries are essential elements in the fabric of his musical embodiments of emotion on the keyboard.

The virginal music of Byrd and the other English masters of the Golden Age and their fantasies for strings marked the beginnings of instrumental music as an independent form of the art; previously it had either accompanied voices (for purposes of religion or for the voicing of human feelings), or dancing for ritual, or marching into battle. But the twentieth century advocates of naked sound matter were not really entitled to claim the practice of Tudor composers as justifying their own counter-revolution against emotion or romanticism;

[1] Vol. V of *The Oxford History of Music*, 1st–3rd editions, pp. 111–12.
[2] *Mozart's Operas*.

in their music for instruments alone, those sixteenth and seventeenth century creators were simply pioneers of the art which was to reach its zenith in the eighteenth and subsequent centuries in a succession of masterpieces of almost infinite variety in the expression of human feelings, moods and aspirations; on this side of their work, they were like the Italian Primitives in painting, who paved the way for the tremendous geniuses to come; but in music for voices, Byrd and his contemporaries in England, Palestrina in Italy, Lassus in the Netherlands, and Vittoria in Spain, were in no sense "primitives", but inheritors of great traditions and creators of glorious masterpieces, whether liturgical in the form of Masses and other settings of the ritual of the Church or secular in the shape of madrigals, ballets and part-songs—all of them either deeply devotional or authentically conveying the emotions of men and women.

Certainly you may find sound patterns in instrumental music of the later seventeenth century and of the eighteenth—in Domenico Scarlatti, for example, and in various movements of C. P. E. Bach and even of Handel, Haydn and Mozart; but so general was the growing tendency to express emotions that for J. S. Bach it was the exception to write a fugue that was a fugue and nothing more: those for organ are majestic monuments of religious faith; the "Forty-eight" fugues traverse an immense range of human feeling; so do those in *The Art of Fugue*—only a few of them are solely due to the fascination which the exercise of sheer contrapuntal skill exerted over this composer. If we are looking for sound patterns in the eighteenth century, we can find the historical record of them in the empty ornaments which singers were allowed to extemporize in the course of the expressive arias composed by Handel in his oratorios; it is a pity to try to reproduce the effect of these today: they were a bad habit, better left in the limbo of forgotten things. They corresponded to the cadenzas which performers were expected to introduce at their own sweet will at certain recognized places in concertos; Beethoven abolished these in his Fifth Pianoforte Concerto, and Elgar, in the Finale of his Violin Concerto, sublimated the cadenza into a glorious memory of previous themes, played by the soloist to a soft orchestral accompaniment. After these splendid examples, surely it is time to give up cadenzas in other works too: they are out-of-date relics of the past, introducing alien thoughts into the composer's fabric, and (I suggest) unwanted by anyone except the person who plays them and who wishes to exhibit his own virtuosity; a very brief flourish or trill could easily take their place, to lead to the genuine music that follows.

II

The greatest music, then, whether we are considering melodies or themes in isolation, or the whole composition of which they form the basis, has become, in the hands of its chief creators, a medium of tremendous range and power for conveying emotion, religion, or thought, for the portrayal of character, and even for the representation of the external, physical world. I have discussed previously[3] in what sense music performs these functions, but I wish here to penetrate a little further into the two last mentioned subjects.

The manner in which music portrays character is unique among the arts. The literary artist can describe a person's nature in the most precise terms, in such a way as to differentiate the individual from all others unmistakably; for he uses the medium by which we normally communicate with one another—words, even though his language may be poetic and thus not that of everyday life. The painter and the sculptor can produce a portrait of a particular man, bearing a close resemblance to a living person, whether the original is real of fictitious. But the musical composer cannot individualize in this way. Music does not actually copy anything in the world outside itself, except in those cases with which I will deal later. It is particularly adapted for expressing emotions—such as joy or grief, pity or anger, love or hatred, regret or triumph, or religious feeling—and the most subtle variations of them; and it can convey qualities, such as courage or serenity of mind, and thoughts, but not theories or

[3] In *The Soul of Music* and *The Divine Quest in Music, passim*. In the following paragraph a little repetition of the ideas contained in the relevant passages of *The Soul of Music* (pp. 24–5, 68, particularly) has been necessary in order to develop them.

arguments. All these subjects of the "language" of music are, however, voiced, as it were, in general terms.

Elgar's *Falstaff* contains one of the most complete portraits of which music is capable; but if he had only called the work "Symphonic Study, op. 68", and had given us no verbal clue, we should never have guessed that it was even associated with Shakespeare's fat knight as portrayed in *Henry IV*. The title, however, was alone enough to enable Tovey[4], with his knowledge of the play and the music, to identify the composer's literary meaning—on the whole, with remarkable accuracy apart from certain discrepancies—when his analysis is compared with that given by Elgar himself in *The Musical Times* of 1st September 1913, which Tovey did not read till afterwards. Elgar describes the opening theme as portraying Falstaff "Not as yet quite absurd but (as Morgann says, writing in 1777) 'in a green old age, mellow, frank, gay, easy, corpulent, loose, unprincipled, and luxurious'." Tovey calls it "the real Falstaff, wallowing, protesting, and formidable in his absurdity". The two accounts are not so very far apart; but they leave untouched the problem *why* a theme consisting, as regards rhythm, mostly of a succession of dotted crotchets followed by semiquavers—with its variety chiefly in its intervals—should convey that character to our minds at all. And the answer is to be found in the fact that music is an independent medium which speaks to us in general terms and is felt to be appropriate, for example, to Falstaff as we know him from the play, once we are given the clue that the composer was seeking to portray him. Similarly, the theme of Prince Hal is, as Tovey says "noble"—courtly and genial, in its first form, as Elgar points out; but we only recognize it for the Prince because it occurs in a work called *Falstaff:* intrinsically, it simply expresses nobility. Diana McVeagh[5] is right when she says, in effect, that Elgar portrays the better side of Falstaff, ignoring or glossing over the baser and lewder side of his nature. But in all these musical portraits, the character-drawing is necessarily generic, not individual. Verdi typifies Iago's sly, sinister character by means of slow-moving, entwining melody. The handling is masterly, just as Wagner's

[4] *Essays in Musical Analysis*, vol. IV, pp. 3–16.
[5] *Edward Elgar*, pp. 172 ff.

use of dropping intervals and part of a descending scale to convey the evil of Hagen is masterly. But in none of these cases should we know that the composer had in mind a particular individual with a literary origin, if we had not been told so by means of words. Mendelssohn wrote in a letter to Frau von Pereira (Genoa, July 1831): "Notes have as definite a meaning as words, perhaps even a more definite one", and in a letter to Souchay (15th October 1842) he maintained that music is not too indefinite to be put into words, but too definite; that words are susceptible of a variety of meanings, while music has only one. Even as great a Mendelssohn enthusiast as Grove, in referring to these letters[6], calls this "so strange a doctrine, which, though true to him, is certainly not true to the majority of men, and which obviously rests on the precise force of the word 'to mean' (*heissen*)." Mendelssohn is, indeed, I think, the only person who has made such a claim about music; I doubt whether anybody agrees with him!

This broad, generic nature of music's representation of those things that exist apart from itself, is seen also in its portrayal of the external world. Just as it cannot "individualize" human characters, so it cannot "copy" concrete objects or events, incidents, or even sounds, unless the latter happen to consist of regular vibrations like music itself. It can, for instance, imitate certain bird's notes, but it can only suggest the movement of a brook; and it does this partly by rhythm. Mussorgsky in *Boris Godounov*, Act I, scene 1, depicts the movement of Pimen the monk's pen across the parchment, as he writes his history of Russia, by means of an "andante molto" figure with legato semiquavers passing up and down, and we sense at once how apt the device is; but if we were not seeing Pimen at work, or had not been told that he is writing, we should not guess that the music represents anything of the kind. It is only in this generalized way, and with this qualification, that we can accept Mussorgsky's own claim[7] that his music is realistic. And when we hear of the *verismo* of Verdi's operas—and of those by other Italian composers—we can only interpret *verismo* as being contrasted with those operas which are based on symbolical or

[6] Grove's *Dictionary of Music and Musicians*: Grove's own article on Mendelssohn in the 1st, 2nd and 3rd editions (3rd edition, vol. III, p. 426). [7] See M. D. Calvocoressi: *Modest Mussorgsky*, pp. 86 ff.

mythological subjects—a matter to which I shall return later. No opera can truly be very "realistic": people in real life do not normally express their emotions and thoughts in song or recitative, nor do they stop to sing love duets or farewells when every moment of delay would in actuality endanger their safety or even their lives; but when this sort of thing happens in opera, we tacitly suspend our disbelief and respond to the conventions of the art-form. Opera in this way is even more remote from real life than poetic drama; Shakespeare was entitled to say, through Hamlet's lips[8], that it is the actor's function "to hold the mirror up to nature", in so far as the dramatist's character-drawing and the basic issues are concerned; but the choice of words which the author of poetic drama uses for the purpose differs from that of everyday existence; in this respect many prose plays approximate much more closely to real life, but opera, even of the *verismo* type, is further away from it than any of these art-forms, and is none the worse for that.

III

The assumption that music expresses emotion has by no means been universally accepted by philosophers. On the contrary, Harold Osborne, for example, attacks it vigorously in his book *Aesthetics and Criticism*. "One man", he says, "describes a piece of music as 'gay' and another finds the same piece 'melancholy', one calls it 'heroic' and another 'tender' . . . the differences between them are not due to poverty of the language" —which "is adequate to show that they do genuinely differ" . . . "There is nothing intrinsically impossible in supposing that music should provide a more delicate and exact system for symbolizing the subtleties of affective life than the very crude instrument afforded by verbal language. . . . But the supposition breaks down on facts. For in order to be effective as symbolization music, or any other system of symbols, would have to signify the same thing for everyone—or at any rate to all those people who were able to use it for the purpose of symbolic communication. . . . There has been experimentation in the last

[8] *Hamlet*, III. ii.

hundred years directed to showing that this is indeed the case with music; but the results of experiment have consistently shown the opposite."[9]

"Musical compositions do not represent or symbolize anything other than themselves. They neither mediate nor suggest any experiences apart from those aural occurrences which *are* the compositions."[10]

"In instrumental music there is no represented emotional content, no element of 'life' emotion; there is only the aesthetic emotion directly aroused in you by the pattern and structure of musical sound which *is* the music."

Harold Osborne was criticizing Susanne K. Langer's theory of artistic symbolism, as put forward in her book *Philosophy in a New Key*. But meanwhile she has developed that theory in its sequel *Feeling and Form*, from which I quote the following passages:

"The tonal structures we call music bear a close logical similarity to the forms of human feeling—forms of growth and attenuation, flowing and stowing, conflict and resolution, speed and arrest, excitement and calm, or subtle activation and dreamy lapses—not joy or sorrow perhaps, but the poignancy of either and both—the greatness and brevity and eternal passing of everything vitally felt. Such is the pattern, or logical form, of sentience; the pattern of music is that same form worked out in pure measured sound and silence. Music is a tonal analogue of emotive life." (p. 27).

"Our interest in music arises from its intimate relation to the all-important life of feeling, whatever that relation may be. After much debate on current theories, the conclusion reached in *Philosophy in a New Key* is that the function of music is not stimulation of feeling, but expression of it; and furthermore, not the symptomatic expression of feelings that beset the composer but a symbolic expression of the forms of sentience as he understands them. It bespeaks his imagination of feelings rather than his own emotional state, and expresses what he *knows about* the so-called 'inner life'; and this may exceed his personal case, because music is a symbolic form through which he may learn as well as utter ideas of human sensibility." (p. 28).

[9] *Op. cit.*, pp. 105 ff. [10] *Op. cit.*, p. 179.

"Music is a significant form, and its significance is that of a symbol, a highly articulated sensuous object, which by virtue of its dynamic structure can express the forms of vital experience which language is peculiarly unfitted to convey. Feeling, life, motion and emotion constitute its import." (p. 32).

Harold Osborne does not sufficiently or definitely differentiate between two questions which are entirely distinct from one another: (1) whether the listeners regard music as itself expressing emotions, and (2) whether it causes them to experience emotions. I believe that the answer of most people would be "yes" to the first question and "no" to the second one.

Fundamentally, an aesthetic theory which is true for one branch of music must be true for another. In practice, almost every composer who has set words to music has composed for them music which he at any rate intended and believed to be expressive of the emotions and meaning contained in them; and we judge his greatness or his talent *partly* by the degree of success with which he does so. Now, music set to words does not differ, basically, in kind, from instrumental music, and at least from Beethoven onwards composers themselves have frequently marked their instrumental scores with expression marks, showing that they regarded their own music as conveying various life-emotions. Think of some of those used by Beethoven alone—"Maestoso", "teneramente", "dolce", "vivace", "deciso", "calmo", "con grand' espressione", "molto espressivo", "Arioso dolente", "Mit innigster Empfindung", "grazioso", "Appassionato e con molto sentimento", "Allegro risoluto". Other later musical creators have followed suit. Now, composers are often not good critics, because they are too much absorbed in their own work to be able to see things from the angle of other composers; but, if Harold Osborne's theory is to be believed, they did not even understand the nature of their own art, and moreover most of the critical writing and speaking about music that has been produced would be reduced to nonsense. Nobody with any musical sensitivity at all could think the lively Finale of Haydn's Symphony No. 102 in B flat to be "melancholy", or fail to sense the spiritual triumph voiced in the last movement of Beethoven's Fifth. Characteristically, Harold Osborne refers to the fact that the opening notes of this symphony were by arbitrary association conventionally symbolized as hope and confidence in victory in World War II, instead of "fate knocking at the door"; but this was only made possible partly by taking the first four notes alone, which are scored in unison, so that it is only later in the theme that the minor key is established for our ears[11], and partly because that war-time association was addressed to a much wider audience than ordinary music lovers —to an audience many of whom would not have in their minds a conscious or even subconscious acquaintance with the remainder of the theme or of Beethoven's movement.

Harold Osborne[12] quotes C. P. E. Bach's assertion: "Since a musician cannot otherwise move people, but he be moved himself, so he must necessarily be able to induce in himself all those effects which he would arouse in his auditors; he conveys his feelings to them, and thus most readily moves them to sympathetic emotions". He contrasts[13] with that these words of Busoni, to show "the change in aesthetic outlook which has come with fuller understanding": "Just as the artist, if he is to move his audience, must never be moved himself—lest he lose, at that moment, his mastery over the material—so the auditor who wants to get the full operatic effect must never regard it as real, if his artistic appreciation is not to be degraded to mere human sympathy". Harold Osborne does not seem to realize that both are partly right. A composer cannot portray emotions without experiencing or at least vividly imagining them, but he does not experience them *at the same time* as composing: he "recollects them in tranquillity", as Wordsworth said a poet does (and as Harold Osborne agrees happens in the case of poetry), and then expresses them in his work; but they must *have been* real to him.

IV

The expressive power of music has been enhanced by the development of instrumental resources in the course of time;

[11] Tovey (*Essays in Musical Analysis*, vol. I, pp. 38–40) pointed out that the whole theme extends for more than twenty bars.
[12] *Op. cit.*, p. 143. [13] *Op. cit.*, p. 165 n.

but the pianoforte is not an "improvement" on the harpsichord: it is merely different, and suited to different music. The virginal pieces of Byrd and the other Elizabethan masters sound better on the harpsichord, as do the sonatas of Domenico Scarlatti. And if we find that the *klavier* music of J. S. Bach goes as well on a modern piano as on a harpsichord, that is partly because he was in advance of his epoch in musical mentality and partly because the universality of his outlook was so tremendous, so fundamental, that it transcended the question of the particular keyboard instrument on which it is to be played.

The valve-horn is an advance on the hand-horn, and the cylinder flute is an improvement on its predecessors. The orchestra has become an infinitely more powerful and subtle medium than it was before the days of Berlioz. Fresh types of instruments have been added to it, and with this huge enlargement of the orchestral palette it has been possible for composers to widen the range of music and to explore the by-ways of psychological expression and of poetical description in ways which were not open even to a creator with the stupendous imagination of Beethoven or to one with the delicate fastidiousness of Mendelssohn, even if they had wished to pursue them. Pathological regions of the mind and character of human or fictitious beings, and the most exquisite nuances of landscape or fancy, became within the scope of music. Richard Strauss's delineations of the nature of Salomé, of the life and adventures of Don Quixote or Till Eulenspiegel in the terms of an elaborate, yet cunning orchestration; Debussy's pictures of clouds and waves and the sun and shadows of trees by means of subtle instrumental effects; Delius' vision of the mountains in *A Song of the High Hills,* conveyed by soaring orchestration in contrast with a wordless chorus to express humanity, and the melting harmonies of his various orchestral landscapes; the richly coloured musical fairy tales of Rimsky-Korsakov and Stravinsky and the latter's brilliant portrayal of the grotesque in *Petruchka;* Alban Berg's narration of the story of Wozzeck through the medium of painful dissonances and weird instrumentation; the tang of the sea in Britten's *Peter Grimes* and the morbidity of the central character; all these, and many other examples that might be quoted, show the manner in which music has enlarged its boundaries even beyond the gorgeous or delicate instrumental pictures of Berlioz or the glowing colours and immense range of Wagner's world of imagery.

This in itself is a form of progress. Yet, paradoxically, it does not follow that the art which results is more beautiful, or more imbued with a spiritual character. For this purpose it is the intrinsic quality of the music that matters, not the extent of its kingdom. It will not profit the art to gain the whole world, if it loses its soul.

Beauty is not the prerogative of any one epoch more than of another, and the existence of a spiritual quality in music does not depend on period, but on the individual genius of particular creators. Side by side with certain psychopathic compositions produced during the last sixty years, we have had such works as Elgar's *Dream of Gerontius*, *The Apostles* and *The Kingdom*, Holst's *Hymn of Jesus*, Sibelius's Seventh Symphony and *Tapiola*, Kodály's *Psalmus Ungaricus*, Vaughan Williams's *Job*, *Sancta Civitas*, *Dona nobis pacem*, Mass in G minor and Fifth Symphony, Bloch's *Sacred Service*, and Britten's *Ceremony of Carols*, *Rejoice in the Lamb* and *Spring Symphony*—revealing either a spiritual character akin to that of the masterpieces of the past or a love of the beauties of nature such as Wordsworth in poetry, Corot, Ruysdael and Constable in painting, or Beethoven and Schubert in music had delighted to convey in days gone by, though using a modern musical palette for the purpose. They may not be on a level with the few very greatest of eighteenth and nineteenth century composers, but there is no trace of a decline in the art of music so long as such composers continue to arise.

The presence of a spiritual quality in a work of art is not enough to ensure its greatness. A composition may possess it in a certain degree, yet not be a creation of great genius, because the composer lacked sufficient technical skill or imagination to give it adequate expression. Another may not contain it, and it may be inappropriate to its subject that it should do so, yet it may be a masterpiece in its own genre: Strauss's *Don Juan* is one instance of this. But those works which combine a high degree of spiritual beauty with supreme skill and tremendous imagination, such as the noblest compositions of Bach and Beethoven, are, I suggest, the supreme achievements in music.

There is no reason why even these two giants should not be equalled in the future; but if so, it will not be because music itself progresses. Musical geniuses, like those of any other sphere, crop up at all sorts of times. The conditions of the age influence the artistic creator, but it is the geniuses that mould the epoch, rather than the epoch that shapes them.

Musical devices may go on being improved in various ways; yet the greatness of the music will not depend on them, but on whether great men are born to produce it, and that is a matter which obeys no laws that historians or biologists have hitherto discovered.

CHAPTER 5

Beethoven's Second Thoughts

"SECOND THOUGHTS ARE best", like so many proverbs, is too sweeping. Sometimes the original idea is the best. And often there are not just two thoughts, but three or four or more in succession. Which is the best, is obviously a question that can only be answered on the merits of each.

Development, alteration, adaptation, of first ideas are methods of creation in every field of activity, but some creative artists naturally employ them more than others. With Beethoven, the constant hammering and chiselling of his first thoughts until they assumed a shape which finally satisfied him, may be seen in the pages of his sketch-books.

In this chapter, however, I wish to deal with two instances which involve something even more far-reaching than that process of constant revision of themes and details—the substitution of a completely new movement, radically different in its materials and in its whole conception. So fundamental a change strikes at the very soul of the work, and is thus directly connected with the main subject of this book.

The first of these cases relates to the Ninth Symphony. The work was completed by March 1824; but though Beethoven had cherished the ambition to set Schiller's *Ode to Joy* to music ever since his youth and had made a good deal of progress with the present Finale, he was apparently still toying with the idea of an instrumental last movement as late as June or July 1823; for a D minor theme for a "Finale Instrumentale" exists among the sketches of that time for the Symphony, but was ultimately used in A minor for the last movement of the string quartet op. 132. And according to Czerny, quoted by Josef Sonnleithner in the *Allgemeine Musikalische Zeitung* of 6th April 1864, Beethoven at some time after the first performance of the Symphony expressed his private conviction to some intimate friends that the vocal Finale was a mistake, and said that he intended to replace it by a purely orchestral one, for which he had already composed a theme.

Now, Verdi thought that the existing Finale of the Symphony is much inferior to the other three movements; but great composers are not always good critics, for they are often too much absorbed in their own art to be able to enter completely into the spirit of another creative artist with a different outlook.[1] Ernest Newman (the *Sunday Times*, 8th April 1956) quoted Verdi with approval, but himself wrote of the "musical magic of the ultimate vocal structure": apparently what he really objected to was the "bridge passage" connecting the Third Movement with the Finale proper: he called the "recitatives" for lower strings "a clumsy device". I venture to disagree. The heavenly dream of the Adagio has been disturbed by harsh discords: (incidentally, how true to life that is!); the ensuing "recitatives" on the 'cellos and basses, and those which follow the references to the earlier movements, are, I suggest, most eloquent; and what they are "saying", so far from being not "manifest" or even "surmisable" until much later (as Newman considered) seems to me immediately as clear as daylight. Beethoven, by the way, is not trying over the themes of the previous movements and rejecting them as unsuitable for his Finale, as is so often stated: he had, of course, no intention of using them for it. What he is telling us is that none of the preceding music *expresses the mood* into which

[1] cf. p. 44.

he now wishes to lead us: the "din" is twice rebuked with dignity, the opening "Allegro" with some impatience followed by a wistful hope of something different, the Scherzo with indignation, and even the Adagio is dismissed decisively, but with a touch of pathos. A premonition of the great theme of Joy appears on the wind instruments, and then the melody itself, beginning softly in the 'cellos and basses, and afterwards gradually taken up by more and more instruments "crescendo", until it is proclaimed by the whole orchestra. A "poco ritenente" phrase, repeated in various keys, almost seems (as Grove said in *Beethoven and his Nine Symphonies*, p. 376) to express the composer's uncertainty or unwillingness to proceed further in his task. And then again we have the "din" that we heard before, but this time it is rebuked by a baritone soloist: Newman complained that the "tones" which the soloist bids us discard include the great Joy theme itself; but surely most listeners interpret the "tones" as referring only to the harsh discords, which have just been repeated with increased emphasis.

Viewed in this light, Beethoven's introduction to his glorious Finale is masterly in its structure and profoundly convincing in its expression. And we should be thankful that he did not obey his "second thought" of using the theme which became the one for the great op. 132 quartet and which is supremely right where it stands but would have been out of place in the Symphony. Consider the first three movements of the Ninth: the storm and stress of the opening Allegro; the vigour of the Second Movement, which is, however, still mostly in a minor key save for the ephemeral happiness of the middle section; the serene tenderness of the Adagio. After this, to have finished the Symphony with a movement based on a theme expressing agitation, in a minor key, would have been a spiritual and artistic flaw. Although we cannot, of course, tell how Beethoven would have treated that theme, the Symphony could only fittingly be ended by a Finale embodying the spirit of Joy. The question whether this should have been vocal or instrumental is an entirely distinct one. Personally, I share the enthusiasm of Tovey and others for the existing vocal conclusion.

The second case is the op. 130 quartet in B flat. In the *Grosse Fuge* (now op. 133) which was its original Finale, Beethoven portrayed the power of the will in a severe strife, though fortified by the tenderness of the "meno mosso e moderato" passages and ending in victory. The majority of his friends found it, as Thayer says[2], "extremely troublesome", and though some of them maintained that it had been misunderstood and would ultimately be appreciated, the others, and above all his publisher Artaria, persuaded him to write a new movement. We who have lived through the horrors of the twentieth century and have learnt to suffer and endure and struggle for the sake of ideals by lessons more bitter than that of the preceding century, have come to understand the beauty inherent in the more austere forms of nature and in the precipices of the *Grosse Fuge*. The substituted Finale did not reach that height, though we may be thankful that in this, his last composition, he was able to create happy music.

These two examples illuminate once more the relationship between music and the world outside itself. For the Finale of the Ninth Symphony the composer chose the theme of Joy and universal brotherhood in preference to any other, not on *purely* "musical" grounds, but because that was the mood which he felt to be the right spiritual climax of his symphony. In the last movement of the B flat quartet he decided to set aside on this occasion the formidable austerities of the *Grosse Fuge* and to rejoice in the less exalted, though cheerful, atmosphere of normal life.

CHAPTER 6

Was Brahms a Conservative?

IT HAS ALWAYS been considered, or even assumed, that Brahms, in contrast with Liszt the pioneer and Wagner the revolutionary, was a conservative. He has even been treated as a "classic"

[2] *The Life of Ludwig van Beethoven*, edited by H. E. Krehbiel, vol. III., p. 222 f.

born out of his time, an upholder of outworn traditions in a romantic, adventurous age, though the superficiality of this extreme view has been realized more recently.

H. C. Colles, a great authority on Brahms, in Vol. VII of the *Oxford History of Music* (1934, p. 63) wrote: "His appetite for adventure was never large, and as life progressed and circumstances forced him increasingly into a position of conservatism, he avoided risks. He could never, like Michelangelo, have produced a David from an imperfect block of marble, or, like Beethoven in the *Grosse Fuge*, have attempted the impossible with four stringed instruments. We shall never know how many failures he destroyed. The long series of great works . . . all bear the mark of this limitation. He speaks that which he knows. They contain no daring escapades of the kind which could make succeeding generations hail him as their pioneer or deride him as a speculator. Brahms is certain and safe. The certainty is his glory. Is the safety to be accounted his shame? . . ."

Richard Specht in his illuminating book *Johannes Brahms* (translated by Eric Blom, p. 89) described the composer as "the custodian of precious possessions". One feature of his music, according to Specht (ibid. p. 95) is that he showed "that great things, nay grandiose and new music could be achieved within the fast and immovable bounds set by the symphonic form consecrated by Beethoven" and he showed that "the more admirably and impressively the closer he traced these bounds".

There are two fallacies, I suggest, in this assumption. In the first place, there were no "fast and immovable bounds set by the symphonic form" when Brahms came upon the scene. Beethoven inherited it from Haydn and Mozart; even in their hands it was an extremely pliable instrument, and one of the manifestations of Beethoven's revolution was that he stretched it almost to bursting point even in his middle period and finally broke the barriers in his third period works: for example, in the Ninth Symphony he introduced a vocal finale of vast proportions; in two of his last string quartets he greatly increased the traditional number of movements; moreover, these final works of his contain vital changes in the internal structure of movements. Secondly, Brahms was an innovator. Quite apart from the profoundly individual nature of his music, the distinctive features or finger-prints which mark the work of all great composers, and the general character of Nordic romanticism which manifested itself in the early part of his life—for example, in the three piano sonatas and the first piano concerto—and never vanished from his art, he introduced important changes into the symphonic structure itself. The characteristic "intermezzo" type of movement, replacing the inherited "scherzo", recurs again and again in his works: in the agitated "allegro molto moderato e comodo" of the C minor string quartet; in the uneasy "intermezzo (allegro ma non troppo)" of the G minor quartet for piano and strings; in the exquisite "grazioso" movements of the clarinet trio (op. 114) and of the F minor sonata for clarinet and piano; in the elegiac third movement ("un poco allegretto") of the string quintet in G, (op. 111); and in the corresponding movements of the first, second and third symphonies; the "un poco allegretto e grazioso" of the first is subdued in tone, and even the liveliness of its alternating section is not whole-hearted; the "allegretto grandioso quasi andantino" of the second is grace itself, yet with a faint undercurrent of melancholy; the "poco allegretto" of the third is equally graceful, but scarcely conceals its grief, which is, as it were, recollected in tranquillity.

Besides this frequent replacement of the "scherzo", Brahms sometimes composed works in three movements, of which the middle one combined the characteristics of slow movement and "scherzo"—an innovation which also occurred to Franck in his symphony: he did this in the violin and piano sonata in A (op. 100) and in the F major string quintet (op. 88). And whereas the traditional form of the concerto had been three movements, Brahms in his second work of that kind for piano introduced an additional one—a scherzo of turbulent character.

It has been suggested that the mere fact that Brahms for the most part employed the symphonic form in his instrumental works indicates that he was a conservative. But that form is not just an abstract structure, into which a composer fits his ideas. It corresponds to something fundamental in human nature—the contrasts of character, the interplay of emotions, the variations of personality, the psychological drama which ends in triumph, in tragedy, or in serenity. That is why it has persisted as a type of composition in so many symphonies, sonatas and chamber music works of vital significance created by Brahms's successors. Brahms had so much to express within the broad and flexible outline of symphonic structure, according to the almost infinite variety of his moods and thoughts, that he had no need to invent a completely new genre for his instrumental conceptions.

In his younger days he was the first of the four signatories of the unfortunate declaration deploring and condemning the principles of the "New German" School, of which Liszt was the leader. This does not prove that Brahms was a conservative: he was no anti-Wagnerian, although his enemies tried to make out that he was; but Liszt's particular brand of musical mentality was repugnant to him and he disapproved of the idea of the symphonic poem—which Liszt constructed out of the prophetic anticipations of it in Beethoven's *Pastoral Symphony* and second Leonora overture. The symphonic poem was, indeed, more obviously a novelty in those days than the new, Brahmsian type of symphony; but subsequent history has shown that there is room for both forms.

In the world of instrumental music Brahms broke fresh ground in two further directions. His Variations on the St. Antony Chorale were the first set of orchestral variations created as an independent composition: previously the variation form had either been used as a movement in a larger work or, if independently, for a solo instrument or chamber music ensemble. And his two overtures were unlike any that had preceded them, but unlike one another in being overtures to nothing: the word "overture" means a beginning, and in the case of Lully's and Bach's overtures (or suites) it really refers to their first number. Brahms's op. 81 is an overture to an unwritten tragedy, created in the form of the first movement of a symphony, but self-contained in its tragic grandeur. The *Academic Festival Overture* is also self-contained, but does not trouble to follow any traditional laws of structure except recapitulation: the only traditional element in it is its adaptation of German student songs, welded into a humorous and genial whole by the hand of a master.

But Brahms's most far-reaching departure from inherited

forms is to be found in his choral music. The *German Requiem* is not liturgical and has no affinity with the traditional Requiems of the Roman Catholic Church except that it is concerned with the theme of death. We may regard it as an oratorio, but it differs radically from all other oratorios composed before or since, in that it is neither dramatic nor narrative in character. All other oratorios followed a story, albeit interrupted by reflective choruses, solos and concerted numbers commenting on the action at various stages. Most of them were settings of tales from the Bible. Handel's *Messiah* was a musical embodiment of Christ's life and Passion and man's belief in eternal life. Even Elgar's *The Dream of Gerontius*, which is the only non-liturgical oratorio either before or since Brahms's *Requiem* entirely concerned with the theme of death and the after-life, treated the subject in the form of a story, set to Cardinal Newman's narrative poem. Brahms's work was unique. Selecting his texts himself from the Scriptures, he conceived it in seven movements, most of which contain in different forms a contrast between darkness and light: sorrow is turned into joy, the transitoriness of earthly life into the eternal happiness of heaven, the vanity of men into trust in God, mourning into comfort, the terrors of death and the Last Judgment into the glory of Resurrection; and at the end the blessedness of those who die in the Lord is set to the same theme as that which in the first chorus told of the blessedness of those who mourn. In type and structure, Brahms's *Requiem* marked as wide a divergence from all choral works that preceded it as Liszt's symphonic poems did from the symphonies of his predecessors.

Brahms also developed a new type of art in his shorter choral works. Schubert, Schumann, Brahms himself, Wolf and others, developed the art of solo song, set to the words of recent poets, with pianoforte accompaniment; Brahms applied the idea to choral music with orchestra. In *The Song of Destiny*, in *Nänie*, in the *Song of the Fates* and the *Alto Rhapsody*, he transmuted the poetry of Holderlin, Schiller and Goethe into shapely musical forms created by his own imagination.

Then again, it was a new departure to compose two (lovely) songs for contralto solo, viola and pianoforte (op. 91) the *Liebeslieder-Walzer* (op. 52) for piano duet and voices (solo quartet) and the *Neue Liebeslieder-Walzer* (op. 65) for four voices and piano. Lastly, the "Four Serious Songs" written at the end of Brahms's life, embodied a novel form of composition: previously, Biblical words had found their expression in church music and oratorio, and songs for solo voice and piano might be religious without being Biblical; the idea of *lieder* set to extracts from the Bible was Brahms's own.

In Britain, the word "conservative" has political associations, and the Conservative party has usually combined a policy of gradual change with adherence to tradition; in the nineteenth century, the reformers were, in the main, the Liberal party. And so, if we are to apply a political metaphor to a composer who lived in that century, perhaps it would not be fanciful to call Brahms a Liberal, rather than a Conservative: he was certainly no revolutionary, but he was something of a pioneer. And the more we reflect upon the subject the more we shall find, I suggest, that the reasons for his innovations lie precisely in his urge to express in new musical forms the emotions, aspirations and thoughts which also exist in the non-musical world.

PART II
INTERLUDE
Music and its Audience

CHAPTER 7

Varieties of Performance

22ND MARCH 1952 was an epoch-making day in the history of the interpretation of Bach in this country. For the first time, the *St. Matthew Passion* was performed here in German in its entirety, by the South London Bach Society at the Church of St. Bartholomew the Great, Smithfield. Eric Blom, confessing that he was not there, wrote in *The Observer* that it struck him as an affectation not to sing so universal a work in the vernacular, and that Bach's instrumental treatment of words does nothing to make his German more comfortable to the music, to performers or to English ears.

Albert Schweitzer has shown how pictorial a composer Bach is, and how throughout his liturgical works musical "motives" recur which are associated with certain dramatic, religious or graphic ideas. This demonstration itself marked a departure from the old conception of Bach as mainly an "abstract" composer, but Schweitzer went further by pointing out that in the recitatives the singer should try to make his effect chiefly by means of the declamatory prominence of the most characteristic words, and should throw single words into high relief. The performance at St. Bartholomew's revealed with what minute attention, particularly in those eloquent recitatives, the composer expressed the meaning of the words of the scriptural narrative in musical terms, and that by comparison something of this intimate connection between text and sounds is inevitably lost when the work is sung in any other language than German. In this respect there is, until Hugo Wolf, no composer after Bach who interprets the significance of words in such detail, with the possible exception of Wagner. Even Schubert usually conveyed the general spirit of a poem, rather than its minutiae, and was unwilling to sacrifice considerations of melody to the faithful following of every word of the text by means of musical expression.

The issue raises again the old question, whether a composition should be performed in the manner that approximates most closely to the conditions of the creator's own day, or in that which makes it more immediately accessible to current audiences. Most music lovers would agree that it is more artistic to sing German *lieder* in the original language of Goethe, Heine and the rest, than in an English translation, however excellent. The ideal method in this country is to sing them in German, if possible with both the German and an English version printed in the programme; (owing to paper shortage or the need for economy, the printing of the German words has sometimes had to be omitted).

No one has suggested, so far as I know, that it is an affectation to sing Wagner in German or that the use of the original languages in the performances at Glyndebourne is misguided. There is, however, a stronger case for performing opera in English than other musical forms: the audience can understand the words (if these are audible) more readily; in a darkened theatre there is no means of following the text in a programme in the original language with a translation, and moreover our eyes should be directed towards the stage; furthermore, the words of the libretti of most operas are less artistic in themselves than the texts to which the great German *lieder*, the songs of Fauré, Duparc and Debussy, or the Bach Passions and cantatas were set. Opera should be given on some occasions in the original language and at other times in the vernacular. Each method has its merits.

The problem, in its wider significance, is, of course, not confined to music. It used to be customary to alter Shakespeare's plays, and even as recently as in the days of Beerbohm Tree the text was extensively cut and great attention was focused on scenic effects. In order to popularize Shakespeare at that stage of the nation's education, this may have been justifiable, but the idea of producing the plays in as complete a version as possible and in conditions more akin to those of Shakespeare's day has grown steadily since then. The filming of Shakespeare to-day is roughly at the same stage as the theatrical production of his plays was in Tree's time. These "cut" versions, with their elaborate settings, at least bring some of the words and dramatic situations of the world's greatest poet and playwright to the minds of millions of people who were not previously very familiar with them. Later on, the cinema public may be ready for more complete and more faithful representations, or, if these are not feasible, may be encouraged by enjoyment of the film to try a more authentic performance in a theatre.

So long as Shakespearean performance is complete, or nearly so, and is well cast and produced, without unnecessary scenery to distract attention from the poet's vivid imagery, there is room both for the modern type of presentation on an ordinary picture-stage and for that which reverts as closely as possible to Elizabethan conditions, such as the productions in the Maddermarket Theatre at Norwich, in the Speech Room at Harrow School, and at the Mermaid Theatre in St. John's Wood a few years ago. Correspondingly, Sir Malcolm Sargent's performances in the Royal Albert Hall of *Messiah* in its entirety but broadly in the conditions which have become traditional in England, can quite well exist concurrently with the complete productions under John Tobin, which both as regards the size of the choir and the use of the instruments revive the practices that prevailed in Handel's time. Tobin has even introduced vocal ornaments which are not to be found in the score that has come down to us, on the ground that the insertion of such devices was customary in those days—though I have expressed the view in chapter four that this is going too far.

Similarly, I suggest that the performance in this country of Bach's Passion music complete in the original language should continue side by side with the complete English version to which the Bach Choir has accustomed us. I am not prepared to say that only one method can be the right one, any more than that Toscanini's conception of Beethoven's Seventh Symphony is alone correct and that those or all other conductors, in so far as they differ from his, are wrong. It is a joy to hear Bach's preludes and fugues on the harpsichord, but to rule out the performance of them on a modern pianoforte at the hands of a gifted interpreter who clearly has an insight into their character, would be to rob the musical world of something which it cannot afford to lose.

The question of cutting raises a distinct issue.

Throughout the nineteenth century and in the early part of the present one, it was the general practice everywhere to ring down the curtain on *Don Giovanni* at the Don's descent to Hell, but the Old Vic won the tributes of the musical world soon after the First World War by restoring Mozart's original comic Finale, and its example has been followed elsewhere since then. In August 1955, however, a correspondent wrote to *The Times* advocating that the opera should end with the disappearance of the Don, on the ground that what follows is an anticlimax, though most of the letters which ensued disagreed with the suggestion.

In the final scene, when the three women, with Ottavio and Masetto, return asking where Don Giovanni is and calling for vengeance on him, Leporello gives a grimly humorous account of the catastrophe, they all settle their future plans, and the sextet ends in a light-hearted fashion, bidding the audience take warning from the Don's fate. Personally, I do not regard this scene as being, *sui generis*, so far inferior to the wonderful music which precedes it but I recognize that opinions may differ on this point. The real issue, however, is that the controversy opens up wider problems than the ending of this particular opera and arises from a fundamental difference of outlook towards the interpretation of musical and dramatic works of art, which, except for those who are content to read a play or are capable of reading a score silently at home, depend on performance for their presentation to the public.

Throughout the work, the situations and emotions have ranged from comedy to pathos and even tragedy and back again, and this composite character is present in the very first scene. But though the opera is really a tragi-comedy, Mozart called it "dramma giocoso" and in his thematic catalogue "opera buffa", and it is obvious that at the time of its composition he did not intend to send his audience away on a note of horror. He cut out the final scene for the Vienna performance of 7th May 1788, but we cannot assume that this excision was meant by him to be permanent.

There is much to be said for the view that there should be no cuts in the rendering of a drama or musical composition, except passages which are generally thought to be spurious, as is sometimes the case in Shakespeare's plays. But whilst it may be reasonable to omit here or there from a long work an aria which is dramatically irrelevant and not remarkable musically, in the course of operas consisting largely of independent numbers and not of the continuous web of sound which came into being in the nineteenth century theatre, the way in which the whole work is to end is clearly of vital importance. Surely, the producer's aim should be to interpret, if not in every detail, the general spirit of the creator's intentions.

If Mozart's comic Finale, which he embodied in the score from the start and left standing in it after 1788, is to be omitted on the ground of alleged bathos, where are we to stop? Is it suggested, for instance, that the happy ending of Gluck's *Orfeo ed Eurydice* should be eliminated because it shows a falling off from "Che faro" and what has gone before, or that the Finale of Beethoven's "Archduke" Trio in B flat should not be played because it is an anti-climax after the sublime Andante? And how can an audience form a true judgment of a composer's or dramatist's work, if it is to be radically altered to what some producers or performers or others think he ought to have written?

The creations of great artists such as Shakespeare, Beethoven and Bach—and others—are universal enough to admit of more than one satisfactory method of interpretation. In a different sphere, they resemble the ideal Forms of Platonic philosophy, which are revealed to the senses in various particular manifestations on Earth.

Nevertheless, radical departures from the composer's completed work are always dangerous. For generations it was the practice to play Beethoven's "Leonora No. 3" overture between the two scenes of the Second Act of *Fidelio*—simply because producers and conductors did not like to deprive the audience of the opportunity of hearing this glorious overture in association with the opera for which it was originally written. But Beethoven knew what he was about when he made his final revision of the opera in 1814, and the insertion at this point of so tremendous a tone-poem (the right place for which ever since then has been the concert room and which embodies the whole drama in its scope) destroys the balance. The *Fidelio* overture is exactly the right prelude before the curtain rises on the First Act—mainly cheerful in character and lighter in quality than either "Leonora No. 2" or "No. 3", though with an element of pathos and anxiety as well, forecasting the middle portion of the opera. The stage action begins with a scene of domestic charm between Marzelline and Jacquino, grows gradually in intensity and grandeur nearly ending in tragedy, and finishes in rejoicing; the final scene naturally relieves the tension after the anguish of the dungeon. No more perfect artistic structure could be imagined. Yet Wieland Wagner thought he could improve on it: he restored the original "Leonora No. 2" in place of the *Fidelio* overture, interchanged the first two vocal numbers to their positions in the first version of the opera, so that the curtain should rise on Marzelline's somewhat pathetic aria rather than on the duet, lighter in quality, between her and Jacquino, substituted mime for all the spoken dialogue—thereby making much of the action unintelligible to those who did not know the opera intimately already—and produced the chorus of prisoners "symbolically" in a pool of light, without Leonora on the stage, though in the actual libretto she is directed to be seen looking among them anxiously and in vain for her husband—a valuable dramatic point in the unfolding of the story. The total result of all this was interesting, but it upset the design. Beethoven and G. F. Treitschke knew better. At Glyndebourne, in 1959, I heard and saw the first authentic performance of the opera, of the many at which I have been present—exactly as it was written by them in the final version; and as the soloists and chorus were first rate, the orchestra the Royal Philharmonic under Vittorio Gui, and the scenery, décor and grouping, and the production generally, a joy to behold, this was far the finest interpretation that I have known: in fact, it was the only perfectly satisfying one.

It remains to consider whether there has been progress in the standard of musical performance.

The human singing voice has not varied in quality throughout the ages as much as the genius of composers has done. You will always find the *laudator temporis acti* assuring you that no female operatic singer has approached the level of Melba since her time. I heard Melba in her prime and in some of her most famous parts, and a lovelier voice, more beautifully produced, could not be imagined. Yet she was a cold singer, and one got the impression that her own singing was more important in her eyes than the expression of the composer's intentions. "I want you to promise," she said to Beverley Nichols[1] "never to hear any other woman sing 'Bohème'." The poor man could only mutter "I promise," but we can sympathize with him at being committed to deprive himself of the pleasure of hearing *La Bohème* after her death. It is indeed possible to conceive (and to recall) warmer interpretations of Puccini's music than hers was. Kirsten Flagstad, though by no means an ideal interpreter of Schubert's *lieder*, had as lovely a voice as Melba's and as well produced, and was a finer interpreter of Wagner than Melba was of Verdi or Puccini. Gervase Elwes was unsurpassed as Gerontius: Heddle Nash and Richard Lewis have equalled him.

Allowing for relatively unimportant variations in the quality of voices and of vocal technique at different periods, solo singing, as such, does not seem either to have progressed or declined in the course of musical history, and it is improbable that choral efficiency has done so in the last few hundred years; we do not know enough about the choirs of antiquity to form an opinion.

So far as the playing of instruments is concerned, most epochs have had their great virtuosi. My grandmother used to tell me how wonderfully Anton Rubinstein performed the Beethoven sonatas, though "he often came down bang on a wrong note". She, however, recognized the greatness of Busoni's playing of them, and with him there were no wrong notes. In my view, Lamond, Schnabel, Myra Hess, Solomon, and Denis Matthews have attained as high a level as Busoni in the interpretation of Beethoven. I knew an old woman who set Paderewski on a pedestal—"no one could touch him at Chopin". I agree that nobody has surpassed him as a performer of the works of his great compatriot, but I place him no higher than Pachmann, Cortot or Horowitz; and like Pachmann he was not

[1] *All I Could Never Be*, p. 61.

remarkable, or even satisfying, when he turned his attention to other composers for the pianoforte. Paganini was regarded in his day as something almost supernatural in the world of violinists; I refuse to believe that he was greater than Kreisler, just as I hold that Menuhin—when he is at his best—and Isaac Stern have attained to Kreisler's level as an artist. Soloist interpretation simply varies from one period to another according to the mysterious, or fortuitous, emergence or non-emergence of individual talent.

Orchestral performances in the twentieth century, even allowing for variations in merit between one orchestra and another, are undoubtedly finer than they were during the first half of the nineteenth century. Beethoven would have been astonished at the level of interpretations of his great masterpieces that we have experienced, if he could have heard them. In Wagner's day matters improved, but even Richter's renderings of his scores did not always satisfy him. We can imagine that these composers would have rejoiced at what has been accomplished under such conductors as Mahler, Nikisch, Toscanini, Bruno Walter, and Klemperer. The improvement in orchestral performance is in no small measure due to the emergence of virtuoso conductors, though we rightly object when a conductor attaches more importance to the exhibition of his own powers than to the interpretation of what he must (if he is sincere) believe to be the composer's true intentions.

CHAPTER 8

Programmes

MANY YEARS AGO I wrote an essay comparing the perfect concert programme with a certain walk which a friend and I had done in Devon and in which Nature seemed, almost deliberately, to have combined unity of design with a rich variety of beautiful scenery.

This still seems to me the ideal scheme for an evening of music, which should be multifarious without incongruity. But I confess that in the intervening years I have widened somewhat my choice of masters whose works can suitably form a one-composer programme. I used to feel that Bach, Beethoven and Wagner alone stood the test. Nowadays, I believe that excerpts from Wagner's operas in the concert room should be confined to whole scenes and overtures, excluding the usual unsatisfactory snippets; and I have learnt by experience that the works of other great composers besides those three can stand up to the ordeal of a one-composer concert, provided that the choice is made judiciously. For instance, the last three symphonies of Mozart, a Chopin recital, songs by Schubert only, or —among moderns—a carefully selected programme of music by Elgar or Sibelius, Bloch or Holst, Delius or Vaughan Williams, may give complete satisfaction.

Of course there has never been any difficulty about the single composition which occupies a whole evening: its unity should, and usually does, sustain our interest; it is the necessity of switching our attention from one composer to another, or even from one work to another, that requires careful planning.

Planning! That is the question! Why must a mixed pianoforte recital usually begin with the eighteenth century, proceed to Beethoven, continue with Chopin or Schumann or Brahms, and end up either with Liszt or a modern group? Tradition, I suppose, or very roughly chronological order—both of them bad reasons. I would begin with a modern group or Liszt and end with Beethoven. The sonatas of Beethoven are still at the head of all music written for the pianoforte, it is not fair to other composers to play their music after them, and Beethoven—not Liszt or Debussy or the charming Spaniards or the interesting moderns—is the satisfying culmination of a recital.

The programme of the Promenade Concerts have improved immeasurably since the old days, when shop ballads appeared in the second part. But ever since World War II sometimes they have been too long, and have contained incongruities. The length of a concert should be about two hours at the most—

unless it consists of a single work such as an oratorio, Mass or cantata, which happens to last longer. The interval should be normally and roughly in the middle—in any case not three-quarters of the way through. Musical indigestion is bad for people of all ages. Even in recent years we have been given the most unsuitable combinations. One-and-a-half hours of Bach have been followed by Mahler's romantic, though childlike, Fourth Symphony. After a lengthy Bach-Handel selection, we have had a strange, new game in sonorities and antiphonies by Goffredo Petrassi and, finally, Ravel's *Bolero* ! New compositions should, I suggest, be sandwiched in between those of well-established, fairly modern, composers, with due regard to intrinsic congruity and not too near the finish of the evening. And what sort of programme-building was it to perform Ravel's single example of a mere musical stunt at the end of a scheme mainly devoted to Handel and Bach?

Above all, there are some things which must end a programme—the closing scenes from *Die Walküre* and *Götterdämmerung,*[1] the "Great C major" of Schubert and the Ninth Symphony of Beethoven. At the Proms. this has now been done in the case of Verdi's Requiem and *The Dream of Gerontius*—each of which really ought to stand by itself. Some people go so far as to say that the Ninth Symphony (which lasts about one hour and ten minutes) should be performed alone in its glory; this is, probably, too much to expect at a Prom.; but surely no music at all, however great, however noble, should come after it. With the Finale of the Ninth, the last musical word has, or ought to have, been spoken—for the evening.

[1] The last scene of *Götterdämmerung* came at the *end* of a Prom. programme for the first time, I think, in 1960.

PART III

MUSIC, DRAMA AND DANCING

CHAPTER 9

Reactions to Ballet

OPERA HAS BEEN called a composite art-form by its friends and a hotch-potch or a hybrid by its enemies. At some stages of its history the dramatic side of it has assumed greater prominence than at others, but the discussion of an opera as a work of art has always been regarded as the function of a musical critic: décor and scenery were important in Wagner's eyes, but the libretto has always ranked second only to the music, and it has been tacitly assumed that a musical critic or any intelligent music lover is a person of sufficiently wide culture to be capable of a reasonably informed opinion of the merits of the libretto; words are the normal means of communication between human beings, and even though they may be in verse and though dramatic criticism is also a separate and specialized craft, appraisal of a libretto does not depend on technical knowledge to the same extent as does criticism of dancing.

Ballet—an art as composite as opera—requires a specialist in the finer points of dance movements and choreography to assess its value, and he may have no great knowledge of music, although the latter plays so vital a part in the whole; whilst few musical critics know enough about the technique of dancing to be able to give an expert opinion, unaided, about the complete product as a work of art. The reactions of those who are ballet "fans" but are not immensely interested in music apart from the ballet, must obviously differ from those who are music lovers. To the former, the music is often simply a background (hence the tendency to interrupt the performance by applause); whereas the music lover cares for the way in which the music, particularly if it is the work of a great composer, is interpreted in terms of dancing, mime, choreography, and so on. One musical acquantance of mine finds that at the ballet his attention is automatically concentrated so much on the music that he is almost oblivious of what is going on across the footlights and has even been known to shut his eyes! It is rare to find anyone sufficiently gifted, and with a wide enough knowledge of the various elements which make up the whole production, to be an ideal member of a ballet audience.

To many a ballet critic or enthusiast who is not specially musical, Frederick Ashton's *Symphonic Variations* is a perfect creation: the patterns of the dancers, the grace and interplay of their movements, the elegance of the décor, all serve to yield exquisite delight. Moreover, even a musician welcomes the complete harmony between the bodily movements and César Franck's rhythms. Yet the ballet does not otherwise fit the music: Franck's score is, in turn, mysterious, romantic and joyous; but the choreography has not enough variety to match it, and is cool, abstract and unemotional; the white dresses and the pale green back-cloth are inappropriate to the warm, colourful strains allotted to pianoforte and orchestra.

Les Sylphides approaches much nearer to a perfect marriage between music and dance: indeed, Fokine's inventions are beautiful interpretations of all the Chopin pieces, even though some of these were not composed in normal dance rhythms. Yet the ballet as a whole has one grave artistic flaw: Chopin's is essentially pianoforte music, and no sensitive music lover, surely, can listen with equanimity to its tranference to an orchestra, however skilfully this may be done—as by Glazunov in this instance. The same applies, in nearly the same degree, to the *Carnaval* ballet: this is a charming production, delightfully in harmony with Schumann's romantic and imaginative work, but not even Rimsky-Korsakov's cunning orchestration overcomes the blemish of removing the music from the pianoforte medium for which it was written and for which it is so ideally suited. Yet if these two ballets were danced to the original pianoforte scores, the audible thump of the dancers' feet would mar our pleasure.

Ashton's *Nocturne*, based on Delius's *Paris*, suffers from a different kind of defect from any of these: although no question arose of any rearrangement of the score, it does not attain to the close interpretation of the music in terms of dancing which *Les Sylphides* and *Carnaval* reveal; nor is it so utterly out of keeping with the general character of the composer's work as the *Symphonic Variations* ballet. Nevertheless, it is an incomplete realization of Delius's composition. Music deals with generalized emotions, and Delius in his poetic vision evoked something of the soul of the great city in music which is at times dreamy, at times sombre; but the ballet seems to narrow it down, as it were, to an expression of the emotions of the poor flower girl, the rich girl, and the young man whose fancies stray from one to the other—with the spectator and the group of revellers forming a kind of background to the pathetic story. It is too limited in its subject and its scope for the wide, far-reaching spaces of the composer's imagination. Delius's mind, as revealed in this score, is too big for the highly individualized experiences of the dancing participants, charmingly though these have been conceived and however touchingly they may be performed. This is a problem which is always liable to recur, because of the generalized nature of the emotions which music conveys, as compared with the concrete, visible expressions of human feelings which dancing, like painting, gives us. It is one which Massine overcame to a large extent by creating *Choreartium* as an abstract ballet, without a story, for the music of Brahms's Fourth Symphony. On a less ambitious level, Balanchine did the same with Bizet's Symphony in C. And it is more successfully faced by John Cranko in his ballet *The Shadow* than it was by Ashton in *Nocturne*: the idea of a girl whose love for a young man is frequently interrupted and threatened by a shadowy figure, but who by her constancy ultimately dispels the shadow and wins her happiness, is sufficiently universal in itself to enable it to be harmonized with the generalized emotions inherent in Dohnanyi's music. We are not conscious of a disparity between the score and the choreographic scheme as we are in *Nocturne*, and we are far away now from the jarring incongruity of *Symphonic Variations*.

There are some ballets in which all the ingredients seem to be integrated into a perfect whole: the two Tchaikovsky masterpieces, *The Sleeping Beauty* and *Swan Lake*, and in later generations *The Three Cornered Hat*, *The Firebird*, *Petruchka* and *Job*. Neither the balletomane for whom the music is a background, nor the music lover who claims no great insight into the art of dancing, nor the ideal spectator and listener who seeks for a perfect blend between music and dance, should have any aesthetic quarrel with any of them. *Petruchka,* has, indeed, been described as the perfect ballet ensemble; and so far as objective criticism can go, I would be disposed to agree. My own personal taste in works of art is in favour of beauty, and for this reason *Petruchka* is not one of my favourite ballets, for there is little opportunity for graceful dancing in it, the movements of the "puppets" are designedly (and rightly) grotesque or even ungainly, and are appropriately matched by dissonant music, albeit interspersed with much that is brilliant, vivid, witty, and ingenious. Apart from some of the costumes of the crowd, there is little that is actually beautiful in *Petruchka*—either for the eye or for the ear; but art does not always, or necessarily, aim at beauty, and *Petruchka* is a perfect study in the grotesque—with a dash of symbolism in it. For beauty and wit combined, in a Spanish setting, we turn to *The Three Cornered Hat* with Massine's choreography and Falla's enchanting music; for the magic of fairy tales realized in a nineteenth century idiom we go to *The Sleeping Beauty* and *Swan Lake,* and in a later manner to Fokine's and Stravinsky's joint creation *The Firebird. Job* embodies the beauty of the Old Testament story in a vision inspired by Blake's glorious pictures, matched by Vaughan Williams's noble, yet dramatic, music.

In all these "perfect" examples, the creators of the ballet and its music have collaborated; so they have in *The Prince of the Pagodas,* which is mostly enchanting to see and hear but is imperfect because it is too diffuse; Cranko spins out his final divertissement unnecessarily, and Britten, with his wonted facility, obligingly goes on composing! And so too, in another Cranko ballet, *Antigone,* where the austere, but moving, spectacle is matched by Mikis Thedorakis's music—at times dissonant, at times diatonic and even gentle.

There are very few completely satisfactory ballets based on pre-existing music: either an ill-fitting story is tacked on to music with a different programme, as in *Scheherazade,* or cold choreography is hitched to warm music as in *Symphonic Variations,* or essentially pianoforte music has to be dolled up in an orchestral dress as in *Les Sylphides* and *Carnaval.* For really great ballets in the future, we depend on great composers arising with a genius for this form of art, in harmony with the imagination of those who devise the visual elements.

CHAPTER 10

Operatic Symbolism

OPERAS HAVE BEEN divided into "tragic" and "comic", "grand" and "light", "seria" and "buffa", "opera" and "music drama" —though this last distinction is not fundamental, for all operas, even comic ones, are really music dramas. Operatic symbolism, however, merits particular attention, and in this chapter I propose to consider its nature and in what sense and to what extent some operas are mainly symbolical in character, whereas others are realistic.

In a wide sense, all music is symbolical. The *Oxford Dictionary* tells us that a symbol is a thing that stands for, represents or denotes something else by vague suggestion or by some accidental or conventional relation; especially a material object representing or taken to represent something immaterial or abstract. The *Encyclopaedia Britannica* defines it as "the term given to a visible object representing to the mind the semblance of something which is not shown but realized by association with it". This definition is not wide enough, for it apparently limits symbols to visible things. Albert Schweitzer (*J. S. Bach*, translated by Ernest Newman, vol. II, p. 15f.) sees that all art speaks in signs and symbols, though this is less noticeable in poetry and painting, since the language of each is also that of daily life. "In music", he says, "the expression is wholly symbolical. . . . It is wrong to imagine that so-called pure music speaks a language that is not symbolical, and that it expresses something of which the meaning is unequivocal. It too appeals to the hearer's power of imagination, only that it is concerned more with abstract feeling and abstract beauty of line than with concrete expression". Suzanne Langer (in *Philosophy in a New Key*) develops the theory of symbolic transformation of experiences as the basic process in the human brain, and says that music at its highest is clearly a symbolic form, albeit an unconsummated symbol, in that the actual function of meaning, which calls for permanent contents, is not fulfilled: it is a significant form, though without conventional significance.[1]

As music's conveyance of emotions or character is generalized, rather than limited to a specific individual[2], in this sense Schweitzer is right in saying that musical expression is wholly symbolical. Moreover, the notes which music employs are themselves symbols, just as words are.

Nevertheless, we can make a distinction between music which aptly conveys the passions and reflections of the human beings in an opera with a realistic libretto and music which is in a narrower sense of the word symbolical in that it embodies the meaning underlying an operatic allegory. It is the distinction, for example, between Verdi's *Rigoletto* and Wagner's *Ring*, between Puccini's *La Bohème* and *The Midsummer Marriage* of Michael Tippett.

Throughout operatic history this contrast has persisted, but it is not rigid: no operas have been entirely symbolical (except in the wide sense of the term mentioned above, under which all musical expression is so); even in *The Ring* there are direct expression of human emotions and graphic representations of nature, in addition to the more mysterious unfolding of an allegory; whilst on the other hand an opera which is mainly realistic may also have a symbolical or allegorical aspect: *Don Giovanni* is an instance of this.

Opera emerged as a distinct art-form about the end of the sixteenth or beginning of the seventeenth century at the hands of the Italians Peri and Caccini, and the tendency of Italian opera from that day to this has been on the whole away from symbolism and towards the direct expression of human emotions and situations. Symbolism has been characteristic of a

[1] She develops this idea further in her later book *Feeling and Form*.
[2] See chapter four.

minority of operas actually composed and is mostly to be found in the art of other nations. The origin of opera is to be traced to the ancient Greek dramas, in which the choruses were accompanied by instruments and in the dialogues either parts were sung or else the actors' voices rose a little above a sing-song, slightly enhancing the inflexions of speech; and the Greek tragedies were largely based on mythical subjects with symbolical or religious associations. The other main source from which opera developed was the medieval liturgical drama, in which music played a large part and which was performed in church by priests and choristers: these dramas, embodying scenes chiefly taken from the New Testament, were bound to have their symbolical aspects and their music was partly influenced by the Gregorian style.

It is, therefore, consonant with the origins and anticipations of opera as an art-form that it should, at least occasionally, be symbolical in character. Monteverdi's imagination was inspired by the Orpheus legend to compose expressive music for a story symbolizing love which lasts after death, disobedience to the divine bidding, and final rest in Heaven. The chorale-like theme in D minor, which recurs frequently in the opera, seems to convey the mystical character of Orpheus. At the end, Apollo appears to Orpheus in his despair, at the foot of Olympus, and takes him aloft, and the chorus sing of his apotheosis. The prevalence of ancient Greek myths as subjects for serious opera up to the time of the French Revolution did not, however, usually cause Italian or French librettists and composers to imbue them with symbolism. Neither Lully nor Rameau can be said to have done so.

Gluck set Greek mythical subjects to French or Italian libretti, but was himself a native of the Upper Palatinate; and of his five greatest "Greek" operas the two earliest have symbolical ingredients. In *Orfeo ed Eurydice* none of the three persons is an ordinary human being: Orpheus, whether he was originally a god of darkness or the liberator from the power of darkness by his gift of music, is in the opera a mysterious character who is able to descend into the nether regions; we first see Eurydice as a ghost in the Elysian fields, and her resumption of human form in order to return to earth as a woman is tacitly assumed; whilst the third character is a divine being, Cupid, the god of love. All these facts combine to suggest a symbolical atmosphere, and the music of the netherworld in Act II enhances it: Orpheus begs the Furies to admit him. They sternly and repeatedly answer "No". He continues his entreaties and they finally yield, their voices sinking to a pianissimo with deep notes on the orchestra. In the Paris version of the opera Gluck introduced the magnificent music of the dance of the Furies from his ballet *Don Juan*. Musical symbolism enabled the composer to depict the terror of Hell in this scene of tragic grandeur, and the peace of heavenly happiness in the serenely beautiful music of the Elysian fields.

The story of *Orfeo ed Eurydice* symbolizes a husband's love for his wife, so complete that he was willing to penetrate the regions of death in order to restore her to life. That of *Alceste* is equally symbolical: it tells of a wife's devotion to her husband, which impelled her even to sacrifice her life in order to save him from death, but is eventually rewarded by reunion with him. The solemn overture, the music in the first Act to which Alcestis prays to the gods to relax their harshness, her decision to offer her life to them in place of her husband's, her impressive aria of invocation to the "Divinités du Styx", are full of religious symbolism. Moreover, the original and more idealistic Italian version of the opera contains a scene in Act II in which Alcestis calls upon the gods of the netherworld, and Death replies by telling her to descend with him after bidding farewell to her husband Admetus and her children; and this version, by omitting Euripides' character of Heracles (who in the later Paris version rescues her from death in gratitude for Admetus' hospitality) makes Apollo restore her to Admetus in thankfulness for his having received him when banished from Olympus and as a reward for their marital devotion.

These two operas show how Gluck's imagination, at this stage of his life, was haunted by myths symbolizing love so faithful that it will face even death for the sake of the beloved one.

In the operas of Mozart, the trombones, which in his day were associated with the Church rather than with the theatre, have a supernatural symbolism. At the end of *Idomeneo* their solemn tones accompany the voice of the oracle. In *Don Giovanni* they are heard in the accompaniment to the words of the Commendatore's Statue in the cemetery and again in the awe-inspiring music of the scene with the Statue in the Don's house—music which, without the trombones, is foreshadowed in the overture. Indeed, this climax of the opera is essentially symbolical: it shows how villainy and unbridled self-indulgence without concern for others, bring their own punishment: the grip of the Statue, the thunder, and the devils that carry off Don Giovanni to the flames of Hell, are religious symbols, consonant with medieval Catholic belief and reflected in Mozart's powerful music. He called his opera "dramma giocoso" and much of the earlier music in it is true to that description; but the sextet of the other main characters after the Don's violent end, though it restores the spirit of comedy, does not efface the tragic and symbolical grandeur of the music that precedes it.

The solemn hymn to the sun for chorus and orchestra, which is the first number in Mozart's incidental music for Gebler's play, *Thamos, König in Aegypten*, also includes a part for trombones. In *Die Zauberflöte*, however, they appear in the score throughout, but express mysticism rather than the supernatural awe which they conveyed in the earlier operas.

Freemasonry itself employs rites and symbols, and in this last opera of Mozart's it is in turn symbolized by the membership of a temple in which Isis and Osiris are worshipped; moreover, certain resemblances between Calderon's *El Purgatorio de San Patricio* and the libretto of the opera (pointed out by Ann Lapraik Livermore in an article in *Music and Letters*, January 1955) indicate a Christian association. Thus *Die Zauberflöte* might be said to be symbolical in a triple sense; and both words and music are in keeping with this strong character of symbolism. The overture opens with three solemn chords in E flat, which recur in B flat in the first Temple scene of the Second Act when the priests give their approval to the initiation of Tamino and Pamina and which thus have a Masonic significance. The Queen of the Night—although in the First Act it is her three ladies who attribute to the magic flute the power of protecting Tamino and of enabling him to bring happiness to his fellowmen—typifies the forces of evil. So, in his grimly comic way, does Monostatos. Her mighty aria in the Second Act is one of the most tremendous embodiments of hatred in the history of music. Contrasted with these emblematic figures of darkness are the representatives of Virtue, Justice, Humanity and Wisdom in the persons of Sarastro, the Speaker of the Temple, the Priests, the two Men in Armour and the three Genii; and the solemn music allotted to them is appropriate to their symbolical character; whilst the melody on the flute, which is played as the lovers pass through the ordeals of fire and water, to the accompaniment of soft notes on the trombones and gentle drum-taps, is a perfect musical symbol of the process of purification.

There are some religious elements and passages in the operas of Beethoven, Weber, Berlioz and Verdi; but unless we place a symbolical interpretation on the music of the Wolf's Glen in *Der Freischütz*, the next great exponent of operatic symbolism after Mozart is Wagner, whose stage works from *Der Fliegende Holländer* to *Parsifal*, with the notable exception of *Die Meistersinger*, are steeped in symbolical associations. The central idea of *Der Fliegende Holländer* is redemption by love. The redemption motive figures in the overture, reappears in the opera, and is, as it were, idealized into an apotheosis both at the end of the overture and at the close of the whole opera, when the spirits of Senta and Vanderdecken after death assume visible shape and are seen rising to Heaven. The Dutchman has symbolized the type of man who has committed blasphemy, Senta the woman whose devotion to him is strong enough to prompt her to sacrifice her life in order to redeem his soul.

The idea of redemption recurs in different forms and degrees in *Tannhäuser*, *Lohengrin*, *The Ring* and *Parsifal*. In *Tannhäuser*, sacred and profane love are symbolized by Elizabeth and Venus. Tannhäuser symbolizes the man who is torn in conflict between them and who gains salvation after death by the sacred love of a pure woman. Thus the Pilgrims' song, the accompanying theme of the "Pulse of Life", the main themes associated with Venus, the music of Elizabeth's entreaty on Tannhäuser's behalf, all have a symbolical significance.

Lohengrin did not obtain redemption by a woman's love, as the Dutchman and Tannhäuser did; but, like them, he aimed at it and sought a woman who would love him without question and never ask him whence he came or his name and race. He was a knight of the Holy Grail, with all its mystic symbolism, which is represented by the etherial music of the prelude and recurs, as does Lohengrin's own motive of knighthood and purity, at various times throughout the opera; both reach their climax in his narration in the Third Act.

Tristan and Isolde is not just a tragic love story. The characters may not be symbolical, but in the words and, still more eloquently, in the music, "Day" is regarded by the lovers as their enemy and symbolizes this world with its lies and deceits, and "Night" represents the eternal world of true everlasting love. It is this mystical symbolism which inspires the exalted character of the music of love and death.

In his First Sketch for *The Ring* Wagner presents three rival forces, each with its symbolic significance: the race of Giants symbolizes foolish, self-centred indolence; Alberich the dwarf, the thirst for wealth and power; and the Gods, the divine wish to save mankind both from Alberich's foul designs and from the lazy materialism of the Giants. When Wagner came to embody his immense scheme in a music-drama for actual performance on the stage, it lost some of its symbolic character: two Giants do not represent an entire race of them, and no beneficent intentions of the Gods towards humanity are reflected in the character of Wotan. Nevertheless, both the music and the drama portray the evil influence of gold, the overthrow of an unworthy pagan theocracy, the greatness of heroism, and redemption by love.

In *Parsifal*, evil paganism is symbolized by Klingsor; Christianity, by Parsifal himself; temptation, by the Flower Maidens. The Grail is represented by Wagner (following a later addition to the original story) as the cup of the Last Supper and the vessel in which the blood of Jesus from the wound caused by the spear was preserved. Kundry has been prevented from serving the Grail because she is under Klingsor's spell through having tempted him. Amfortas has been wounded by Klingsor with the sacred spear and can only be healed by a touch from it. The work is steeped in religious symbolism from start to finish.

It is in connection with *Parsifal* that Ernest Newman[3] wrote that the beauty and profundity of its prelude made Nietzsche conscious . . . that, in a work of art, only the art matters, not

[3] *Wagner Nights*, p. 710.

the body of knowledge or system of thought with which it happens to be conjoined. "The fact that we do not believe in ghosts does not make us shut our ears to *Hamlet;* the fact that the gods of the Greeks are not ours does not make us abuse the Greek dramatists for falling at the feet of Zeus. . . . A work of art like *Parsifal* is to be accepted in virtue of the appeal it makes to the artist in us, whether we are Christian or Jew or freethinker. This or that theological of philosophical 'answer to the problems that disturb us' (. . . Nietzsche's words) is valid for one of us and invalid for his neighbour, but art has no concern with these things; and to fulminate against *Parsifal* for the Christianity of its subject is, even for the freethinker who happens to be also an artist, as absurd as it would be to turn our backs on the *Divina Commedia* because we have no belief in the medieval theological system that was accepted as the final truth by Dante. Art of itself has nothing to do with 'truths' of the material world that are true for one man, one sect, but false for another. . . . The 'truth' of art and the 'truth' of life are entirely different things. Poetic truth, said Aristotle, 'should not be confused with truth historical, logical or moral'; and Philodemus of Gadara, writing in Rome in the first century B.C., laid it down that in poetry anything and everything can be 'true', 'including themes fabulous and even false, monsters or legendary spirits, provided they are artistically represented, in concrete and vivid fashion'."

I am sure that all this is true. But I suggest also that there is a *symbolic* "truth" transcending all these "truths", and that in the Ghost in *Hamlet* (even if we do not believe in ghosts), and in the gods of the ancient Greeks and in Christian doctrine (even if we do not accept all of it as our personal religion) and in Wagner's *Parsifal* story itself, we can recognize symbolic "truths" which are just as real as historical truth and that of everyday life and are, also, distinct from, and more comprehensive than, the strictly "artistic" truth to which Ernest Newman here refers. Most people do not regard the creation story in Genesis or the tale of the valley of dry bones in Ezekiel as being literally, historically true: but in addition to their purely *artistic* truth—for both the Hebraic and the Authorized Versions of these Old Testament books are great literature—we can believe in their *symbolic* truth: the first chapter of Genesis is a perfectly credible symbolic account of Creation; and the thirty-seventh chapter of Ezekiel is a credible presentation, in symbolic form, of faith in the resurrection of the "spiritual bodies" of men.

There are religious ingredients in the operas of Gounod, Bizet, Massenet and Saint-Saëns, and there is religious history in Mussorgsky's *Boris Godounov* and *Khovanchina;* but symbolism re-entered the opera house in the present century. Holst's *Savitri* is a musical setting of a Hindu story of the triumph of a woman's love for her husband over Death, who is personified as a character on the stage. In Busoni's *Doktor Faust,* quite apart from the religious, and indeed Christian, passages, the dead child of Faust and the Duchess of Parma is actually the symbol of his will, though he does not realize this at first. In the last scene, he sees the figure of Christ crucified, but it changes into that of Helen of Troy. He declares that there is no grace in Heaven, but, before dying, transmutes his life and his will into the dead child. In both these operas, the symbolism is reflected in the mystical character of the music. For *Ariadne auf Naxos* Richard Strauss composed a lovely score; yet Ariadne's final acceptance of the love of Bacchus in place of Death is represented by music which is, indeed, idyllic, but misses the symbolism of Hofmannstahl's conception.

Benjamin Britten imparts a Christian symbolism into the story of *The Rape of Lucretia* in both the words and the music of his Prologue and Epilogue. Hindemith's *Mathis der Maler* discovers a symbolical triumph of spiritual forces in the tale of the painter who joined in the unsuccessful revolt of the peasants against oppression and ultimately leaves his patron's employment to go into the world, alone, relying only on his genius and the tools of his craft.

Vaughan Williams's "morality", *The Pilgrim's Progress,* is as full, musically, of Christian symbolism as were the written words of Bunyan's masterpiece. The discords and orchestral colours of "Vanity Fair" and the dissonances which accompany Apollyon's utterances are contrasted with the serenity and exaltation of the "celestial" parts of the work.

Michael Tippett (in a series of articles in the *Observer,* in the autumn of 1952) has told us that in *The Midsummer Marriage* he took a "prim' uomo" and a "prima donna" whose illusions were, so to speak, spiritual; to match against a "second' uomo" and soubrette whose illusions were social; so that the eventual marriage of the first pair became a spiritual, even supernatural, symbol, transcending the social and biological significance of the eventual marriage of the second pair. At the beginning, Mark, a warm-hearted, amorous young man, is rebuffed by Jenifer, a cold, hard young woman; but in Tippett's words, "the magical archetypes take charge": the girl rises to a "heaven" and the man descends to a "hell", but these are really forms of ordeal and purification, and ultimately the pair are transfigured. In footnotes to the libretto, Jenifer's transformation is said to correspond, in Greek myth, to the motherless birth of Athena from Zeus's head, and that of Mark to the second birth of Dionysus, son of the earth-born Semele, from Zeus's thigh. The stage appearances are idealized in the mystical music which reveals the transfiguration of Mark and Jenifer in lustrous tone more fully than words or theatrical lighting. The two "ancients" who are priest and priestess of the temple, and the oracular figure of Sosostris, who is described only as a clairvoyante but proves to be an instrument of revelation, enhance the symbolical aspect of the opera. King Fisher, the worldly father of Jenifer, who lays sacrilegious hands on Sosostris, is stricken to death, and the young couple are united in idyllic happiness. Whilst the music of the ritual dances is complex, as befits the strange character of the dances themselves, the music of the transfiguration and of the happy ending of the opera is lucid and essentially simple.

Werner Egk's *Irische Legende* is based on the story of Countess Kathleen O'Shea: she sold her soul to the Devil to rescue the Irish peasantry from starvation owing to famine and to save the souls of those who had already bartered theirs for gold, but at her death God took her soul away from the Devil because of the nobility of her self-sacrifice. The music does not, however, rise to the height of this fine, symbolical subject.

An opera is no better for being symbolical rather than realistic. *The Ring* is not a greater masterpiece than *Die Meistersinger*, nor Gluck's *Orfeo* than Mozart's *Figaro*. But whilst Richard Strauss has probably gone as far as a composer can in depicting the psychology of individuals, it is pre-eminently the province of music to convey generalized emotions and ideas. It is, therefore, peculiarly well-fitted, with its far-reaching power of suggestion and reference, its mysterious undertones, its use of leading motives and other means of expression, to carry a symbolical message; and operatic symbolism is a natural growth in the musical universe.

CHAPTER 11

Electra in Drama and Music

ON ITS WAY to the Trojan War, the Greek fleet assembled at Aulis was prevented from sailing by an absence of wind, for Agamemnon, commander-in-chief of the combined forces, had offended the goddess Artemis by slaying a hind sacred to her and boasting that he was a better hunter. The prophet Calchas announced that her wrath could only be appeased by the sacrifice of Iphigenia, one of the daughters of Agamemnon and Clytaemnestra. Thus the fleet was able to sail. After the defeat of Troy, Agamemnon returned home at last to Mycenae, where his kinsman Aegisthus had seduced Clytaemnestra. Together these two murdered Agamemnon, Clytaemnestra's motives being her illicit love for Aegisthus, her wrath at the death of Iphigenia, and Agamemnon's own infidelities.

The story of Electra, another daughter of Agamemnon and Clytaemnestra, is told by Aeschylus in the *Choephorae*, ("Libation-bearers"), the second drama of his Oresteian trilogy, and by Sophocles and Euripides in the separate plays which bear her name. It tells how Electra and her brother Orestes avenged their father's death by killing Aegisthus and Clytaemnestra, but the three Greek dramatists treat it in divergent ways, and Hofmannstahl's version, in his libretto for Richard Strauss's opera, differs from all of them.

In Aeschylus, the characters in the whole trilogy are presented as instruments of superhuman forces, Vengeance, Pity, Justice and Reconciliation, and Electra in the *Choephorae* does not dominate the action as she does in Sophocles and Euripides; Orestes, if anything, plays a more important part than she does; after the deaths of Aegisthus and Clytaemnestra, she does not speak; and it is Orestes alone who is haunted by the Eumenides, (the Furies, who are symbolical embodiments of vengeance). This ending links the play to the concluding drama of the trilogy, in which the Eumenides continue to pursue Orestes but are finally pacified by the goddess Athene, he is acquitted by the Athenian Court of Justice, and the whole story ends in harmony and reconciliation.

In Sophocles, too, the killing of Clytaemnestra is treated both by Electra and Orestes as a dreadful act of justice and piety, to avenge the murder of Agamemnon. When Orestes and Pylades go in to do the deed, Electra prays to Apollo—

> Be Thou the gracious helper of our plans,
> And show to all men how the Gods bestow
> Their due rewards on all impiety.
> (E. H. Plumtre's translation, vol. I, p. 238).

On hearing Clytaemnestra's cry after the first blow, Electra calls out—

> Smite her yet again,
> If thou hast strength for it.
> (ibid. p. 239)

—but that is to ensure that Clytaemnestra is killed, and not merely wounded. Electra is ruthless, but she does not gloat over the deed. And Orestes kills Aegisthus, as the play closes, simply because—

> Doom like this
> Should fall on all who dare transgress the laws,
> The doom of death. Then wickedness no more
> Would multiply its strength. (ibid. p. 243)

Orestes is not threatened with the punishment of being haunted by Furies; a new life, based on the affection of brother and sister opens up before them; the blood-curse of the house has been laid to rest; justice has been done.

In Euripides, Aegisthus does not appear; we only hear of his death, which is spoken of as an act of retribution. The killing of Clytaemnestra is regarded both by Electra and Orestes as an appalling act of justice which they are impelled to carry out, though it is Electra who urges Orestes to do the deed. So far from glorying in it, Orestes is horrified at it and Electra's first words after it are—

> Much to be mourned, my brother, to be mourned
> With tears, and I the cause. Unchecked, unawed
> I to my mother came, I boldly came
> To her that gave me birth. Alas thy fate,
> Thy fate, my mother! Thou hast suffered ills,
> And from thy children, whose remembrance time
> Can ne'er efface, deeds ruthless, and far worse
> Than ruthless: yet with justice hast thou paid
> This debt to vengeance for my father's blood.
> (Robert Potter's translation, Everyman edition of Euripides's Plays, vol. I, p. 192.)

Then Castor and Pollux appear and give Electra in marriage to the good Pylades: Orestes, they declare, must pay the penalty of matricide by being haunted by the Furies, but ultimately he will be absolved from the doom of blood in the great judgment court on the mount of Ares at Athens: here Euripides follows Aeschylus in ending the tragic story on a note of forgiveness and reconciliation.

How different is the treatment of the subject in the Hofmannstahl-Strauss opera! In her opening monologue, Elektra looks forward with blood-thirsty eagerness to the glorious moment when those who murdered Agamemnon will in their turn be pouring out their life-blood on his tomb, together with that of the horses from his stables and the dogs that formerly licked his sandals, while she, with her brother and her sister Chrysothemis, will be dancing the royal dance of victory around the tomb. At the end of the monologue the music anticipates the dance to which she is looking forward. And the opera closes with a dance of triumph, as Elektra, whose reason has snapped in her exultant joy, gloats over her victims in a wild, musical blood-bath and eventually falls lifeless.

Ernest Newman (*Opera Nights*, p. 147) tells us that "the tremendous expressive apparatus of modern music has . . . made possible to librettist and composer a beauty at the very heart of horror that was beyond the scope even of the finest minds of the ancient world". And in the *Sunday Times* (21st December 1952) he invited "the classical student . . . to ask himself whether music here, as in so many instances in opera, has not soared sometimes far above and plumbed far deeper below the best that poetry can ever achieve". Similarly, Noel Goodwin, in an article on *Elektra* in *Musical Opinion* (May 1953), wrote: "the miracle of music has enabled the composer and librettist to find an element even of beauty at the core of horror, and here, as in so many great operas, music can inspire heights of emotion and depths of feeling which even the most beautiful poetry can never hope to reach".

No one could justly accuse me of being insensitive to the effects of music, but I do not agree that the greatest heights and depths of emotion are beyond the scope of poetry. And the view that the *Elektra* of Hofmannstahl and Strauss discovered a beauty at the heart, or core, of horror that was beyond the reach of the great Athenian dramatists is, I suggest, difficult to accept. One of Strauss's chief contributions to the art of music was that he explored psychopathic recesses of human character and emotions to an extent to which no composer had done before him, and he found a medium for them in the elaborate orchestral apparatus developed from Berlioz and Wagner. His obvious interest in the morbid and sadistic elements of human consciousness and subconsciousness found full scope in the Hofmannstahl version of the Electra story, as it had done previously in Hedwig Lachmann's adaptation of Wilde's *Salome*. Strauss was more successful in painting the struggles of the sick, dying man in *Tod und Verklärung* than the Transfiguration which followed them; he was adept at portraying the pranks of Till Eulenspiegel, the oddities and insanity of Don Quixote; he portrayed in masterly fashion the sadism of Salome, selecting this of all Biblical subjects. It was characteristic of him that he should glory in an Electra who danced exultantly at the murders of her victims and then fell down dead in her insane exhaustion. But marvellous though his performance in this opera was, can it truthfully be said that it contains a beauty higher and also more profound than the great achievements of the Greek poets mentioned earlier in this chapter? The art of Euripides, it is true, for all his genius, marked in the main a certain falling-off from the exalted heights of his two great predecessors; but in his *Electra* there is a beauty of treatment which is, surely, on a loftier plane than the psychopathic sadism of Strauss's score.

As Ernest Newman pointed out in another *Sunday Times* article (17th May 1953), the Wagnerian *leitmotiv* enabled Strauss to achieve the double function of reminiscence and foreboding which the Greek dramatists, particularly Sophocles, fulfilled by means of their famous "tragic irony", and in *Elektra* the Recognition Scene between sister and brother, which is the emotional core of every drama on the subject, is a scene of great and moving beauty. But the use of the *leitmotiv*, however masterly, does not necessarily mean that the actual music is transcendent, and G. Wilson Knight has shown how recurrent images in a play of Shakespeare help to create a "universe" which, I suggest, enables poetry to plumb the depths and scale the heights as potently as music can and to possess the evocative power of the *leitmotiv*. Moreover, one scene, however beautiful, cannot redeem a whole opera, any more than one swallow makes a summer.

Strauss was, indeed, a great composer; but there are degrees of greatness. Aeschylus and Sophocles, even if not Euripides, are among the few supreme creative artists of the world—commensurate in stature with Homer and Dante, with Michelangelo and Rembrandt, with Shakespeare and Goethe, with Bach and Beethoven. We can appreciate the genius of Strauss, and the mastery and beauty of *Elektra*, without going so far as to place him on a level with (or apparently even above!) some of the most exalted poets, and whilst recognizing that, for all his power and imagination, his art lacked the grandeur of spirit which is present in the work of the world's greatest artistic creators.

CHAPTER 12

Great Tragic Music-Drama

ARISTOTLE IN THE *Poetics* said that a tragedy is "an imitation of an action that is serious, complete and of a certain magnitude . . . effecting by means of pity and fear the purgation of these emotions"; also, that an unhappy ending is the right one. Yet, though he calls Euripides "the most tragic of the poets", he admits that it is only "many", not all, of his tragedies that end sadly. Elsewhere, he expressly says that a tragedy may have either a happy or an unhappy ending, and that it should deal with a "serious" action (there is no exact English equivalent for his adjective) and should be "dignified". Tragic personages should be "good"—"better than the ordinary man", by which he means above the common level; the poet, in representing men with defects of character, should preserve the type and yet ennoble it.

The *Oxford Dictionary* defines tragedy as (1) a play or other literary work of a serious or sorrowful character, with a fatal or disastrous conclusion, and (2) that branch of dramatic art which treats of sorrowful or terrible events, in a serious and dignified style. The first meaning would disallow the happy ending, though the second was perhaps not intended to do so entirely.

Tragedy began in Greece, and is thought to have sprung from the Dionysian ritual of Vegetation, which ended in an epiphany or resurrection. Hence it is not surprising that some Greek tragedies ended more or less happily, either through the intervention of a *deus ex machina* or by a final reconciliation or harmony. This was not confined to Euripides.

I suggest that, whilst accepting pity and fear as two of the main emotional ingredients in tragedy, we should not completely rule out the happy ending; and that for a drama to be worthy of the name "tragedy", it should possess, in some form, what we may call "tragic grandeur", and that this in turn requires that one or other of the protagonists should be a person who, at the outset, either possesses some element of nobility of character or of position or both; the story will often consist in his or her degenerating from that height, possibly as a result of temptation either from within or without, and meeting with death at the end. If a play or opera consists only of sordid characters, or if its hero or heroine is merely pathetic, it scarcely deserves to be dignified with the name of "tragedy", or anyhow of "great tragedy".

The phrase "music-drama" dates from Wagner and differentiates his mature works, with their "unending melody" and their tissue of subtly changing leitmotives, from his earlier operas, which still retained to a large extent set pieces—arias and concerted numbers—like those of his predecessors. But intrinsically it is applicable to any work which is at once musical and "dramatic"—unfolding a plot by means of characters who (unlike those in ballet) use words as well as action. All the operas that have ever existed, whether serious or light, are in this sense "music-dramas", though "drama" has in modern parlance come to be associated less with the latter than with the former. There is, therefore, no reason why "tragic music-drama" should be thought to have begun with Wagner. Any opera which has the true qualities of tragedy can be so described.

I propose to consider how these ideas justify us in applying the term "great tragic music-drama" to some works and not to others; but my instances are not, of course, intended to be in any way exhaustive.

The first great tragic music-drama was Monteverdi's *Orfeo*. It is a dramatic and penetrating interpretation, by means of moving melodies and orchestral effects as well as recitative, of the ancient and beautiful story of Orpheus, his undying love for his wife Eurydice, his attempt to rescue her, after death, from the underworld, his failure and grief, and—in this version—his own ascent under the guidance of his mythical father, Apollo, to Heaven, where he will see Eurydice among the stars and live in eternal peace.

In Gluck's opera on the same subject we have the tragic grandeur of the music of the Furies, the celestial strains of the scene in the Elysian fields, and Orfeo's noble expression of grief, "Che faro", in a major key, when Eurydice dies for the second time. Cupid unexpectedly restores her to life, as a reward for his faithfulness, and the joyful dancing and singing at the close are an anti-climax. But neither this, nor the artificial happy ending of *Alceste* where Apollo appears at the last moment and reunites Admetus and Alcestis, nor the feeble, though cheerful, finish of *Iphigenia in Aulis*, need prevent any of these three works from being included here: for until the last episodes, they have been full of the characteristics of great tragedy: in *Alceste*, the sublime overture and prayers to the gods at the imminence of the king's death, Alcestis's invocation "Divinités du Styx", the ensuing, impressive scene (in the Italian version) between her and Death, the dramatic revelation to Admetus of her self-sacrifice for his sake, and his distraction of mind; and in *Iphigenia in Aulis*, the tragic overture, the anguish of Agamemnon, the anxiety, fierceness, and deeply religious feeling of the successive choruses, and the drama of Clytaemnestra's "Jove, dart thy lightning".

Iphigenia in Tauris is the greatest of the series. After the short, peaceful beginning of the overture, tragedy starts with an orchestral storm, in the midst of which Iphigenia raises her voice in a prayer for mercy; and from then onward the pity and terror of the drama, its tale of murder and despair, of pursuit by the Furies, of grief and of threatened human sacrifice, continue almost without respite, save for the mutual recognition of Iphigenia and Orestes near the end, until the last-minute rescue by Pylades and his Greek followers, and are vividly represented by music of tragic grandeur and expressiveness.

Mozart's operatic genius lay mainly in the direction of comedy. *Don Giovanni* is essentially a tragi-comedy; but *Idomeneo*—a late example of "opera seria"—is a tale of threatened human sacrifice (like *Iphigenia in Tauris*), of love and jealousy, of storm and supernatural terror in the shape of a sea-monster; only by a divine oracle at the very end is happiness secured; even so, Electra's jealous love for Idamante has finished unhappily. And Mozart's music is exalted, passionate, and tragic, according to the emotions of the characters and the needs of he drama.

Handel's stage works consist largely of arias and concerted

numbers of great beauty and expressiveness, but a typical Handel opera, though it may have tragic ingredients, is not, as a whole, great "drama". Beethoven's *Fidelio,* a great music-drama, is not tragic at all: its heroic story resembles those of the Gluck and Mozart operas which we have been considering, in being a tense drama with a happy ending; but its First Act opens with a scene of charming domesticity, and from the moment that the trumpet sounds in the dungeon scene, right to the end, the mood is one of ecstatic joy and thanksgiving.

Eighteenth century audiences demanded light-hearted, happy endings. The nineteenth century, turning to a deep romanticism, did not. *The Flying Dutchman, Tannhäuser, Lohengrin, The Ring* and *Tristan und Isolde* are all great tragic music-dramas in our sense of the term, but let us confine ourselves to Wagner's mature works. *Parsifal* is not basically tragic—except possibly for three of the characters, Kundry, Titurel, and—if you like!—Klingsor. It is religious and mystical, culminating in the healing of Amfortas's wound at last, and the assumption of the holy office by Parsifal, who blesses the worshipping brethren as he holds the Grail aloft; the whole of the Third Act is, indeed, permeated by a serene and celestial beauty.

Wagner's greatest *tragic* music-dramas are *The Ring* and *Tristan. Das Rheingold* is a (vast) "Prologue", and *Die Walküre, Siegfried* and *Götterdämmerung* are each described as "music-dramas", but the whole *Ring* is, in truth, one work in ten Acts; we cannot justifiably separate *Siegfried* from the other portions and say that it is not tragic because it contains many cheerful, even humorous, passages and ends with a long, triumphant, love-duet; *The Ring,* considered as a whole, is a gigantic musical tragedy in a pagan setting, though given a Christian twist, not only because it constantly reveals the evil influence of gold and of the desire for world dominance, but because it ends with the redemptive power of human love as the great leitmotiv expressing that idea returns at the close of *Götterdämmerung* and brings the whole cycle to a serene and majestic finish. There has, of course, been tragedy enough before then: Alberich's curse, and the quarrel between the Giants; the tragic love of Siegmund and Sieglinde, the killing of Siegmund (and of Hunding), and the noble grief of Wotan at parting from Brünnhilde; the overthrow of Wotan's power at the hands of Siegfried; and all the tragic events of *Götterdämmerung*, culminating in Siegfried's death and Brünnhilde's self-sacrifice. But Wagner never finished on a note of pessimism; and when he turned to the story of Tristan and Isolde, he not only simplified it but ennobled it into the greatest and most perfect of music-dramas, and gave it a mystical cast which, at the end, when Isolde sings her "Liebestod", reunites her to Tristan in death that is to be eternal life. In Wagner, these two love one another before they drink the potion, which only serves to undo the restraints that formerly checked their love. Tristan unselfishly escorts her to be King Marke's bride, but nothing in the text suggests that she marries the King. The love of Tristan and Isolde is exalted, and is idealistically associated with "Night", as contrasted with the falsehoods of "Day" and the world around us; when Tristan is dying of the wound inflicted by Melot, Marke, who had spoken in sorrow, not anger, to Tristan when he believed him to have been disloyal to him, seeks, too late, to bestow Isolde on him in marriage; and when to these factors we add Brangäne's devotion to Isolde and Kurvenal's to Tristan, we find that the tragedy is indeed mitigated by assuaging elements.

The two parts of *The Trojans* of Berlioz are bound together by the personality and destiny of Aeneas. In *The Capture of Troy*, Cassandra is the tragic heroine, who foretells the doom of Troy, loses her lover Coroebus in battle, and ultimately leads her countrywomen in the sacrifice of their lives in order to avoid a worse fate. Aeneas, at the behest of Hector's ghost, escapes with a band of followers, to fulfil the mission of founding a great city in Italy. The Trojan March, first heard in the major key with tragic irony as the people triumphantly drag in the Wooden Horse, which with its fateful load of Greek soldiers compasses their overthrow, proves in later stages of the drama to be a leading motive that, transformed in various ways and sometimes into the minor, expresses the varying fortunes of the Trojan remnant and their glorious destiny. The music of *The Capture of Troy* has a kind of antique grandeur that is entirely in keeping with its subject. With *The Trojans at Carthage*, a more romantic element enters. Aeneas and his comrades help Dido and her Carthaginians to defeat the Numidian invader, and she and

Aeneas fall in love; their passion is consummated in the climax of the great hunt and storm scene, when they take refuge in a cave from the raging of the elements. Their love music in the peaceful, moon-lit garden, is some of the most beautiful ever created; but Mercury, with his repeated cries of "Italy", recalls Aeneas to his destiny, and from then onwards except for the humorous scene between the two sentinels—the tragedy deepens. Dido cannot grasp that Aeneas is torn between love and duty. In her frenzy and hatred she calls on the gods for vengeance on him and his Trojans, and as they sail away from Carthage she slays herself with the sword that once was his, prophesying that Carthage will perish and Rome become the Eternal City. The Carthaginians burst into curses against the Trojans, but as a vision of Rome appears, the Trojan March is thundered out once more, victoriously, by the orchestra, and the curtain falls. The whole conception is of the utmost tragic grandeur, ending—as so many of the greatest tragedies have done—on a note of spiritual glory.

The plot of *Carmen* might seem sordid, if too briefly summarized; but jealousy, revenge, retribution, the contest between sacred and profane love, are among the themes of some of the world's greatest tragedies. Carmen is an alluring, passionate, heartless, inconstant gipsy. Her courage (like Iago's) is her one virtue. She remains the same person throughout; whereas Don José gradually degenerates under her malign influence. He starts as a decent, soldierly fellow, a good son, idyllically in love with the sweet-natured Micaela; he is captivated by Carmen, yet, on seeing Micaela again, vows his love for her and his devotion to his mother. But he becomes enmeshed in Carmen's net, and, through her, involved in throwing in his lot with the smugglers, for whose life of crime he proves basically unfitted. Micaela tries again to rescue him, and when he hears from her that his mother is dying he goes with her, declaring, however, to Carmen that he and she will meet again in spite of her having rejected his love in favour of the Toreador. When he returns, it is to stab her in his furious jealousy; yet the music-drama does not end at that point: for all the "profanity" of his love for her, there is something almost noble in the resignation with which he bids an officer of the guard take him and confesses that he has killed her, something pathetic in the way in which he flings himself upon her body, protesting that he adores her. The sinister theme which concluded the prelude has recurred in different guises during the action, and is thundered out by the orchestra as the curtain falls: it seems to express the tragic fate which is overtaking José and Carmen too, she herself being the instrument. This is indeed a tragedy of Nemesis.

The Spanish rhythms which abound in Bizet's wonderful music, and the very gaiety and brilliance of some of it, provide the atmosphere in which the whole drama is set. And there are two points in the score in which the soldierly side of José's character is actually *combined* musically with what I may call the Carmen elements. One is the distant sounding of the military retreat on the cornets, which José at once hears, against the fascinating song of Carmen as she dances with her castanets; the other—also in the Third Act—is his passionate, moving, yet courageous phrase to the words "Hélas, hélas, pitié Carmen,—pitié—O mon Dieu! hélas"—whereupon he wrenches himself away from her arms in response to the call of duty.

Boris Godunov is the greatest historical music drama on a tragic theme. The real Boris was not guilty of the murder of Dmitri, the young son of Ivan the Terrible, but Mussorgsky, following Pushkin's play and Karamzin's History, portrayed him as such and presented him as a veritable Russian Macbeth, haunted by visions of the murdered boy and tortured by his guilty conscience: there is even a further similarity in Grigory's alliance with the Poles against him and invasion of Russia, corresponding to Macduff's alliance with the English and victorious march from across the Border against the murderous Macbeth in Shakespeare's play—though of course the parallel cannot be pushed too far.

Boris is a tragedy not only of the King himself, but of the Russian people. In Mussorgsky's original version, there was no Revolution scene; but when he came to write his "second edition", though he left out the scene in front of the St. Basil Cathedral which had preceded that of Boris's death, he conceived the marvellous Revolution scene and sensed that the right place for it was at the end of the opera. In my view, the most satisfactory production that I have seen has been that presented at Covent Garden in the autumn of 1958, when Mussorgsky's own score was used (without Rimsky-Korsakov's unwarrantable alterations) and both the "St. Basil" scene—before that of Boris's death—and the Revolution scene, as the conclusion of the whole work, were performed: both have their places in the music-drama, and the repetition of the lament of the Simpleton, left alone on the stage, for the plight of Russia, is a most effective ending.

Mussorgsky, with his marvellous characterization, his gift of conveying the atmosphere of the time and setting of the drama, his judicious use of leitmotives, his vivid, yet never ornate, scoring, has created one of the most moving and powerful of tragic music-dramas: the hallucination scene in Act II and the scene of Boris's death are tremendous both dramatically and musically; yet the portrayal of the pity and terror which the whole history brings to the Russian people and which Mussorgsky succeeds in presenting so imaginatively, is not less masterly; and the contrasted passages—the music for Boris's children, the Polish scenes, and so on—are cunningly woven into the sombre tapestry without impairing the unity of the whole.

Aïda is pure fiction, in an ancient Egyptian setting. It is a noble tale of love that is true until death, of heroism and conflicting loyalties, of jealousy that repents too late. And it was fortunate that the idea was presented to Verdi sufficiently late in his career for him to be able to treat it not just as an opera in his earlier manner with four-square melodies and set pieces, but as a music-drama in which, though some of the older features still appear, the melodic tissue is far more continuous and developed, the harmonies, rhythms and orchestration more varied and enriched, for the expression of the deeply affecting emotions and situations of the tragic story. The love of Radames, the triumphant Egyptian general, for the gentle captured Ethiopian girl who is really the King's daughter, remains constant from its first idyllic expression in "Celeste Aïda" to his final death-song with her. Her love for him is only deflected temporarily under extreme pressure from her afflicted and patriotic father when she is torn between her loyalty to her country and her devotion to Radames—a struggle set to music of great power and poignancy. At the end she joins her condemned lover in the vault, and their last music together, after its initial sadness, rises into the celestial heights of peace. In contrast to these is the complex character of Amneris, with her passion and her jealousy that is ultimately dissolved in prayer for her beloved Radames. The stirring marches and processions, the brilliant pageantry and the dances of the Egyptian girls, effective and appropriate though they are in their places, are relatively unimportant. The real greatness of *Aïda* rests in the musical embodiment of the drama within the souls of its leading personages and the solemn background of the music of the priests and priestesses, with its haunting refrains that are essentially oriental and yet are original in idiom.

In Verdi's *Otello*, the orchestral storm at sea is a fitting prelude to Othello's spiritual storms which are to come later. Iago is a Satanic figure, whose cunning is depicted by winding melodic turns that suggest the coils of a serpent; and his "Credo" expresses belief in a cruel god "who has created me in his own image"—opening with a fierce unison on the orchestra which reappears later with soft, sinister chords. His music alone would be enough to tell us that the hot-blooded, open-hearted Othello and the devoted, innocent Desdemona will fall ready victims to his intrigues. Their love duet is one of the most beautiful in existence, but Othello's jealousy, fiery wrath and brooding dejection are portrayed with equal mastery. Desdemona's infinitely sad "Willow song" and the gentle tones of her "Ave Maria" are followed by the final scene of tragedy; the whole work ends with an almost unbearably piteous reminder of the "kiss" motive from the earlier love duet as Othello falls on her body "to die upon a kiss". If pity and terror and a man's fall from greatness or nobility to death, and possibly even to perdition, are materials for tragedy, then assuredly *Otello* is one of the greatest of tragic music-dramas.

In turning to the twentieth century, we inevitably enter on more controversial ground and on borderline cases. The sad, touching endings of Puccini's deservedly popular and skilful operas scarcely justify their being called "great tragedies": the music of *Tosca* is not dignified enough for that; Mimi and Butterfly are, musically, pathetic rather than great tragic figures. In *Salome*, Richard Strauss selected the most repulsive subject in the history of opera, and his music, powerful and masterly both in technique and in its psychopathic subtleties, is exactly appropriate to this; there was no scope for it to be either "dignified" or exalted. In *Elektra* he found a story which in the hands of the ancient Greek dramatists had been treated with tragic grandeur; but in spite of the impressive "Agamemnon" motive and the beauty of the Recognition scene, he and Hofmannsthal debased the subject by making Elektra blood-thirstily anticipate the blood-bath that is to come and dance gloating over her victims at the end until she falls dead. Musical sadism has hitherto never gone further than in these two operas.

For quite different reasons, I must also exclude *Wozzeck*. The subject is utterly sordid, the characters abnormal to the verge of insanity. Büchner, on whose play Berg based his work, was moved by great compassion for the "underdog", and the composer was too; but during the greater part of the opera, this compassion in Berg's mind for the miserable creatures on the stage and their depressing story is not conveyed to us musically, for the score is harshly dissonant and the characters are enjoined to speak largely in a *sprech-stimme* which is not fully musical at all but mid-way between speech and song and extremely hard on the ear. Almost the only exception to the unpleasant idiom is Marie's meditation and prayer in Act III, scene 1; and the sole occasion on which Berg finds an opportunity to express to us his feelings for all these wretched people in musical terms is in the interlude before the final scene, when he certainly pours out his pity in eloquent orchestral tones. Compassion is a noble thing, but one interlude and one scene are not enough to convert a mainly sordid work, however masterly, into a great tragic music-drama.

I regard Britten's *Peter Grimes* as a borderline case. In the opera, Peter is more pathetic than in Crabbe's poem; but he remains a sadist, and in spite of the loyalty and tenderness of Ellen Orford, the kindliness of Balstrode, and the skill with which the tang of the sea, the tempest, and the atmosphere of the East Anglian fishing village are conveyed in the score, the fact that the whole work is dominated by the musical-dramatic representation of so miserable a creature as Grimes, masterly though it is, prevents me from including it among the great tragic music-dramas of all time.

Janáček's two operas, *Jenufa* and *Katya Kabanova*, both deal with ordinary folk and if we consider the bare outlines of the story in each case, it might seem that a libretto based on it would be sordid; yet it is not so, and the music is anything but that.

Jenufa has a bastard child by a heartless man who refuses to marry her. She is loved by another man, Laca, who jealously wounds her, but repents. Her foster-mother, obsessed by her shame, kills the baby secretly, but when Jenufa is accused of the murder, confesses her own guilt and is led away for trial. Jenufa marries the faithful Laca. Even apart from the music, the drama built on this tale has several noble ingredients. The foster-mother is actuated by love for Jenufa and deep concern for her happiness. Jenufa forgives her and not only forgives Laca but realizes that she returns his devoted love.

In the other work, Katya is victimized by her tyrannical mother-in-law, Kabanicha, and Tichon, her husband, is under his mother's influence and we are told that, when angry, he is cruel to Katya and then drinks and beats her. Thus our sympathy is inevitably aroused for her in her love for Boris, the more so as she is genuinely religious but has yielded to sin in her marital unhappiness. She publicly confesses her adultery, the lovers agree to part, and she throws herself into the river.

The story of both these operas is exalted by its treatment—a thing which would have been impracticable in the case of *Wozzeck* and scarcely feasible with *Peter Grimes;* and the music, tense, terse, moving and powerful, is shot through with a poignant beauty. *Jenufa* is melodic in idiom (with Czech dance rhythms in appropriate places) and contains at times sudden pauses and repetitions of phrases with subtle differences. The score of *Katya* is even more compressed in style, but never grates upon the ear. Janáček needed no twelve-note technique: his original mind found its own idiom in a modern development of the traditional language of music.

These are two great twentieth century tragic music-dramas. Another is Walton's *Troilus and Cressida.* In Christopher Hassall's libretto, the portrait of Cressida is based on Chaucer's, not on the faithless woman in Shakespeare's play. He and the composer have ennobled her character, and thus have romanticized and exalted the story. Her father, Calkas, the High Priest, deserts to the Greeks and succeeds in his demand that she be sent to him under an exchange of prisoners. She vows fidelity to Troilus, and he promises to pass messages to her through the enemy lines, but these are intercepted and destroyed by her servant at Calkas's bidding. Yet she still trusts and loves Troilus, but the servant and Calkas induce her to yield to the Greek Diomede's desire to marry her and make her Queen of Argos, her father telling her that if she refuses he himself will be tortured and she will become a slave and drab like the other captive women. Only under this extreme pressure does she reluctantly give way, though she is also conscious of Diomede's charms. Then Troilus with Pandarus (her uncle) appears, under a truce, as her ransom is being arranged. Troilus begs her to come, but she tells him that it is too late. The Greeks are already pouring in to acclaim her as Queen. When Diomede re-enters, she decides in favour of Troilus and clings to him. In the ensuring fight, he is getting the better of Diomede, but Calkas wounds him mortally from behind. Diomede sends Calkas back to Troy, but says that she must remain as a prisoner without privileges. Rather than suffer this, she kills herself. Thus "false Cressida" becomes a great tragic heroine. And Walton, using his individual utterance that belongs to this century and yet springs from the roots of the past, has embodied the ennobled story in music that is in turn exalted, passionate, and imbued with tragic grandeur.

CHAPTER 13

Great Operatic Comedy

"COMEDY"—"COMŌDIA"—BEGAN in ancient Greece. The word was a compound either of "cōmos" (revel, merry-making) or of its probable source, "cōmē" (village), and "aoidos" (singer, minstrel), from "aeidein" (to sing). And as the last two syllables of "tragedy" are similarly derived from singing, and music played a large part in both types of play, any idea that opera—which originated from the old Attic drama—is a hotch-potch, with music and drama artificially thrown together, or, at best, fused together, is beside the mark. When Peri and Caccini devised the first operas at the beginning of the seventeenth century A.D., they were actually reverting to the types from which drama first sprang—combinations of action in which both speech and music participated: the purely spoken play had been a later development than the Greek "music-drama" of Aeschylus, Sophocles, Euripides and Aristophanes.

Aristotle, in the *Poetics*, says that comedy started with the phallic songs which still survived in his day in many cities. This would connect it with the primitive worship of the male genital organ, as the symbol of fertility, and there was originally nothing ribald about that. For the Athenians, however, a comedy, whether it had sex in or not, was mainly a joke—but not wholly, even in the Old Comedy of Aristophanes: for in his plays there are, besides all the funny bits, many choruses and other passages of great lyrical beauty and charm, patriotic songs in praise of Athens, and so on: they were thus more like the Gilbert and Sullivan operas than the simply humorous or witty ones of Offenbach.

As time went on, "comedy" enlarged its meaning. From being a light and amusing stage play, with a happy ending, it came to be applied in the Middle Ages to other than dramatic compositions—to narrative poems with a happy conclusion, such as Dante's *Divine Comedy*, and to mystery plays or interludes with prosperous endings, such as Christmas plays and those dealing with the temptation of Jesus and the story of Jacob and Esau.

All these elements, satirical, burlesque, simply laughable—with or without malice—emotional and even romantic, gradually became ingredients in comedy, in various degrees and admixtures: wit or humour, and a happy ending, were essential features; but sentiment or romance might even in some cases predominate over laughter.

Now just as the art of Aristophanes, though extremely funny, was also charming, beautiful and, at times, even serious, I suggest that the greatest operatic comedies—like the comedies of Molière and Shakespeare—not only amuse us, but also reflect the emotions of tenderness or pathos—and of course they must end happily. Moreover, they depict characters, whether human or supernatural: the main difference between a comedy and a farce is that the latter depends almost entirely on funny situations, with practically no character-drawing.

Some dramas—such as certain ancient Greek ones, or Gluck's operas based on old Greek myths, or Mozart's *Idomeneo*—which, like comedies, have (more or less) happy conclusions, are nevertheless "tragedies", if they have been tragic in character for most of their length: (this is probably due to Greek tragedy having sprung, as we have seen,[1] from the Dionysian ritual of vegetation, which ended in a resurrection or epiphany). Many plays and operas are neither tragedies nor comedies.

Let us consider instances in which, in the light of these ideas, we may call some works "great operatic comedies", but not others.

Don Giovanni is a tragi-comedy. Mozart called it a "dramma giocoso"; but even in the first scene, the Don kills the Commendatore and thus sets the stage for the nemesis which ultimately overtakes him. There are many comic episodes, and the opera ends with Leporello's grimly humorous account of Don Giovanni's fate and the happiness of the final sextet; but whatever Mozart's original intention, he evidently became caught up in the tragic implications of the story as he went on: not only

[1] p. 90.

did he write pathetic or even tragic music for Donna Anna, but the terrible consequences of the Don's wickedness caused the music to acquire a character of tragic grandeur, first in the overture, then in the cemetery scene, and finally in the banquet scene, when the statue appears and sweeps him off to Hell.

The Magic Flute is neither a tragedy—obviously—nor a comedy: for though certain plays on Biblical subjects with happy endings were called "comedies" in the Middle Ages, to-day we cannot suitably give that name to an opera of such a predominantly spiritual character as this last one of Mozart's in spite of the endearing, homely comedian, Papageno and the half-sinister, half-comic portrait of Monostatos. The solemnity of the music associated with Sarastro and the Temple and its servants, and the whole conception of the ordeals and trials through which Tamino and Pamina have to pass before they ultimately find peace and happiness, are not the stuff of which "comedy" is made, but of a sacred ritual ending in glory.

The greatness of Mozart as a creator of pure operatic comedy is revealed in *Die Entführung aus dem Serail, Le Nozze di Figaro* and *Cosi fan tutte*. In *Die Entführung* amusing entertainment is combined with deep feeling, in the exotic setting of a harem. Osmin, the overseer of Pasha Selim's harem, is a richly comic character who is nevertheless a menace but is ultimately defeated. Pedrillo, the former servant of Belmonte, is the saucy fellow who chiefly causes his overthrow and is also himself romantic at heart. Constanze—appropriately bearing the name of Mozart's future wife—even in her coloratura aria, "Ach, ich liebte", sings of grief and regret for lost happiness and resolve to shun temptation, and in "Traurigkeit" in the Second Act she voices the sorrow she has borne ever since she was forced to part from her lover, Belmonte. In "Martern aller Arten" she resolutely defies the Pasha. We know from a letter from Mozart to his father that the orchestral accompaniment to Belmonte's first song "O wie ängstlich", in which he tells of his devotion to her, was intended to describe the throbbing of the loving heart (first and second violins in octaves), the trembling, the faltering, the heaving of the breast (a "crescendo"), the whispering and sighing (first violins, muted, and flute in unison); there is clearly an autobiographical touch here.

Humour, grief, romantic love, excitement, adventure, and, finally, joy and forgiveness are all portrayed in music of unfailing mastery and beauty. *Die Entführung* is a great operatic comedy, just because its comic spirit and its profound emotions are alike presented with consummate art.

Beaumarchais's play *Le Mariage de Figaro* is a clever, amusing imbroglio of love, female attraction, farce, and political satire. Da Ponte's libretto for Mozart's opera on the same subject follows Beaumarchais pretty closely, but the composer's genius has transmuted it into one of the most beautiful of operatic comedies. His music not only portrays characters, but transcends the work of the librettist and of Beaumarchais himself. Susanna is alert, witty, mischievous, but fundamentally loyal; in "Deh vieni, non tardar" she shows that she is also tender-hearted, romantic and loving. Cherubino is an ardent young lover, very susceptible, agitated, lacking in self-confidence, yet happy: he reveals all this in the music of "Non so piu"; in "Voi che sapete" he voices the delight, the torment, the turmoil of love, in universal terms. The Countess is the dignified lady, of good manners, who knows of her husband's infidelities, yet remains unembittered; but her heart nearly breaks in the deeply pathetic, almost tragic, emotion of "Dove sono". The tangle of intrigue, of "torments, caprices and follies", is resolved in the last scene, when, in the enchantment of a summer night in the garden, the Count in moving "andante" tones begs her to forgive him, she does so in phrases of great tenderness, and all the characters join in an ensemble of rejoicing. Beaumarchais had satirized the arrogance of an aristocrat, even though he did not envisage the political anticipations of the French Revolution which were attributed to his play; he was chiefly concerned to amuse his audience. Mozart amuses us too, but he does much more than that: he deepens the characters, introduces far more emotion, and transforms the ending from a conventional resolution of a series of mistaken identities into a Finale of reconciliation and happiness.

Although the plot of *Cosi fan tutte* was said to have been taken from an actual event that had recently occurred in Vienna, at the suggestion of the Emperor Joseph II, who commissioned the opera, da Ponte's libretto is completely artificial and even symmetrical. The scene is Naples. There are two sisters, two young officers engaged to be married to them, and two conspirators. The officers, in pursuance of a bet with Don Alfonso, a cynical old bachelor friend, that their fiancées will remain faithful to them, pretend to have been called away to join their regiment, but return disguised as Albanian noblemen. Alfonso is helped by Despina, the ladies' maid. Each officer makes love to the other's fiancée, and, after some resistance, is successful. It all ends happily, but whether the sisters are united to their original lovers or to the new ones is not clear, and presumably da Ponte and Mozart themselves did not know; Alfonso says it does not matter: "cosi fan tutte"—women always behave like that! The music chuckles and ripples along deliciously, but it also conveys a wide range of emotions. Sometimes we scarcely know whether to take the musical expression of them seriously or not. For example, in the quintet "sento, o Dio", immediately following the news that the two officers are called up for service, some of the music is comic, but that sung by the ladies is disconsolate. In the next quintet, the couples sing farewell to one another in accents of pathos voiced by most beautiful music, while Alfonso laughs in the background. Dorabella's grief at Ferrando's departure, in her recitative and aria "Ah, scostati", sounds almost tragic, yet is deliberately exaggerated so as to be a burlesque. And Fiordiligi, in her song "Come scoglio", expresses her rock-like constancy, but it is obviously a paradoy, with its immense leaps and wide intervals. *Cosi fan tutte* is not a farce, but a great operatic comedy. Its lovely music blends wit, humour and satire, with emotion—whether genuine or artificial. It does not rely on amusing situations, but portrays human character.

Rossini's *Il Barbiere di Siviglia* is inevitably set side by side with Mozart's *Figaro* because both are based on Beaumarchais plays, the story of the Mozart opera being the sequel to that of *Il Barbiere*. Both are richly comic and witty, and if we say that Mozart's far surpasses the other work, we are merely reflecting the obvious fact that he was a much greater composer. There is really no point in such comparisons. *Figaro* is one of the most beautiful operatic comedies ever written; *Il Barbiere* is one of the most brilliant of "opera buffe". There is very little emotion in the music, partly because the libretto does not call for it; and Rossini's response to any serious feeling in the words—as in the later part of "Ecco ridente" or in "Una voce poco fa"—is by way of an unemotional, though technically exciting, coloratura. The fun and charm of the opera—both its words and its music—are irresistible; and the characters of the principal persons—the vivacious, resourceful, unscrupulous, amusing Figaro, the mischievous, kittenish Rosina, the sentimental, persevering Almaviva, and the amorous old Bartolo, are all mostly deftly portrayed.

The same composer's *La Cenerentola* also is a charming opera, but not one of the greatest operatic comedies. It is not so consummate a work of art as the *Barbiere,* because the "Cinderella" story was less well suited to Rossini's particular gifts. He disliked setting anything that would have been "impossible" in real life; and so in this opera there are no fairy elements, and consequently there is no magic in the score. It is gay and amusing, and not lacking in romance and sentiment; but Cinderella herself, whom we have loved and known all our lives as a most romantic figure, is here a coloratura contralto; and with Rossini, coloratura was not—as it was with Mozart and as ornament was with Chopin—a vehicle for genuine emotion, but only for display.

Beethoven's *Fidelio* and Weber's three greatest operas are neither comedies nor tragedies. *Fidelio* is a heroic music-drama of wedded love, ending in victory. The Weber works are simply romantic operas with happy endings. *DerFreischütz* nearly has a tragic finish, and some parts of it are tragic in character; it also has light-hearted episodes, and at the close evil is overthrown and Max and Agathe are united. *Euryanthe*—an opera with lovely music but a stupid libretto—is also partly tragic, but true love wins happiness in the end. *Oberon* is a fairy tale of love and adventure, but it, too, has no comic elements, with the possible exception of the effect of the strains of Sherasmin's magic horn on the negro attendants in Act III, who, like Monostatos and his slaves in *The Magic Flute*, are made to dance at a critical moment.

Towards the end of his career Berlioz had been ill and

unhappy, and probably welcomed an escape into the imaginary world of a charming comedy. Indeed, in *Béatrice et Bénédict*, based on *Much Ado About Nothing*, he eliminated all the elements of evil, pathos, and stress, which exist in Shakespeare's play. Don John disappears, and Claudio and Hero become merely a pair of lovers who get married. Berlioz concentrated mainly on the story of Beatrice and Benedict. He also introduced Somarone, a new comic character, who rehearses an "Épithalame grotesque" with choir and court musicians for the marriage of Claudio and Hero—in the form of an amusing fugue, because "fugue" means flight and they are to think of the flight of time; and at the beginning of Act II Somarone "improvises" a gay "Drinking Chorus", with guitars, trumpets and tambourines, by way of preparation for the wedding feast. The opera inevitably lacks the drama of the Shakespearean original, but it is full of wit and charm and vivacity in the portrayal of the two principal characters; there is an enchanting, lilting Sicilienne, which reappears as an entr'acte; in Hero's song "Je vais le voir" there are both tenderness and passion, and her duet with her maid Ursula in the evening calm of the garden at the end of the First Act is Berlioz at his most exquisite. In spite of the lack of dramatic tension, *Béatrice et Bénédict* is one of the purest gems in the history of operatic comedy.

Smetana's *The Bartered Bride* is an intensely national opera which has been internationally enjoyed. The gay, light-hearted parts are mainly those in which the people figure, as represented by chorus and dancers, rather than the principal characters: the cheerful chorus of villagers at the beginning; the delightful polka and choral song which conclude the First Act; the chorus in praise of beer at the opening of Act II, the ensuing peasant's dance, and the lively orchestral folk-music which begins the finale of that Act, when the villagers return, and which has been anticipated in the overture; the exhilarating melodies to which the comedians dance in the Third Act, and the rejoicing of the people in the last scene. Much of the music of the leading characters is romantic, pathetic, or at least serious, in accordance with the needs of the story: Jenik and Marenca sing a tender love strain in consecutive sixths, which acts as a recurring leitmotiv throughout the opera; Marenca is at times anxious and even sorrowful in her melodies, particularly in Act III—before the joyful truth of Jenik's identity is revealed to her; and the parents and stepmother are, necessarily, serious in their demeanour and actions, and, therefore, in their music, until the joyous ending. The comic element is provided by Kecal, the marriage broker, with his repetitions and his gabble, on whom the tables are turned at the end, and by the shy, stuttering Vasek, who is, however, rather pathetic in his imbecility. The characteristic, irresistible Czech rhythms of folk song[2] and dance, the fluctuating fortunes of the story and the varied emotions of its music, the humour and the charm of the whole thing, all combine to make this one of the great comedy operas of the world.

Roughly contemporary with these two delightful works is Wagner's great, warm-hearted, genial masterpiece of happiness, love, friendship, and humour—tinged, nevertheless, with melancholy and resignation—*Die Meistersinger*. It shares one important characteristic with *The Bartered Bride*: a combination of intense nationalism with an almost universal appeal. It is German through and through: its glowing, rich, yet never gaudy, nineteenth century score reflects the wondrous beauty of the old city of Nuremberg as it was in the sixteenth century; it concludes with a tribute to "holy German art" which the German Masters have guided and kept noble and German in soul, and an injunction by Hans Sachs to Walther and the populace to continue to honour those German Masters even if foreign kings should come to rule the land. Yet the characters and emotions are common to all humanity, and in sheer range of feeling this opera surpasses all other operatic comedies. We have the tender, ardent love-strains of Walther and Eva, and the touching scenes between her and Sachs; the sturdy, pompous music of the Mastersingers, and the cunning transformation of this into the humorous, light-hearted, chattering phrases of their apprentices; the biting malice of the narrow-minded, pedantic Beckmesser; and, above all, the warm, sympathetic nobility and wisdom of Hans Sachs. The humour is provided by the

[2] I am not suggesting that any of the villagers' melodies are actually folk-tunes; they were all invented by Smetana, but they bear the stamp of Czech folk-music.

apprentices and by Beckmesser, whom the critic Hanslick, Wagner's enemy, had some grounds for treating as a caricature of himself; but it is not a harsh one, and in the opera we are simply amused at Beckmesser's well-deserved discomfiture in Acts II and III, which he largely brings upon himself. In the prelude to the Third Act, in Sach's monologue "Wahn! Wahn!", and at other moments, Wagner reaches more profound depths of feeling and thought than any previous composer had sounded in an operatic comedy: Sach's sad reflections on the madness of the world, his sense of resignation, the love unsatisfied, stronger than mere friendship, which he really cherished for Eva himself, and the solemn music with which he greets Luther and the Reformation. Think, too, of the exquisite nature touches—the "scent" of the elder tree, the serenity of Midsummer Eve; and then the blazing sunshine of the final scene—for the music here surely depicts this, as a fitting setting for the gay procession of the guilds, the dancing of the apprentices, the ultimate triumph of Walther in the Prize-song, the joyful outcome of his and Eva's love for one another, and the final homage to Sachs. *Die Meistersinger* is really unique: it is—in spite of its passages of sorrow and solemnity—a "happy" opera, rather than a "comic" one.

"Great operatic comedy" naturally includes great light opera. And in somewhat the same way as Mozart surpasses Rossini in the sheer loveliness of his music and because of the deeper emotion of his operas, Sullivan and Johann Strauss transcend Offenbach. *Orpheus in the Underworld* (*Orfée aux Enfers*), *La belle Hélène*, and *La Vie Parisienne*, are tremendous fun: they are brilliant burlesques, and the music stimulates and bubbles like champagne: it is all on the surface, there is practically no emotion in it. Yet it is *Die Fledermaus* which ends with a chorus in praise of champagne: this is appropriate enough, but the music of this opera has had more "body" in it than Offenbach's, and more feeling. That is perhaps why it has continued to exert a more potent appeal for subsequent generations. Beneath the lilt of the Viennese waltzes, the grace and exhilaration of the other melodies, the fervour of the Czardas, there is a depth of sentiment which is absent from Offenbach's music. Eisenstein thinks he is flirting with an attractive stranger at the ball; but she turns out to be his wife, behind the mask, and in the end she has the laugh on him. The whole story is a very slight one; it is Strauss's music which brings the characters to life and makes them into credible human beings. And *Der Zigeunerbaron*, with its gipsy girl who turns out to be a princess, its long-lost wife, its love music, is more romantic still, and thus even further away from the merely surface brilliance of Offenbach.

Sullivan is the greatest of those composers who have shone principally in light opera. Yet the wit and humour lie mainly in the librettos: Gilbert's lyrics are brilliant, but when he is at his funniest, Sullivan is often content either to let the words predominate and to provide unobtrusive music for them or to compose music which is itself delightful but does not attempt to be intrinsically amusing: for instance, the words of the sentry's song at the beginning of Act II of *Iolanthe* are Gilbert at his wittiest, while Sullivan's melody is simply charming; who would have thought, listening only to such stirring tunes as "For he himself has said it" in *H.M.S. Pinafore* or Lord Mountararat's song "When Britain really ruled the waves" in *Iolanthe* or the March and Chorus of Peers, that they are set to lyrics which are mainly humorous and satirical? Gilbert, somewhat sadistically, liked to tilt at elderly spinsters, but Sullivan did not attempt to translate this into musical terms: Katisha, for example, is musically almost a tragic figure at her first appearance in *The Mikado*. Sullivan certainly showed his genius for musical humour, as in the entrance of the Lord Chancellor in *Iolanthe* or the orchestral effects which accompany the "execution" trio in *The Mikado*. But he is perhaps even more remarkable for his ability to write music of varied emotions: the vivid power and imagination in the song about "the ghosts' high noon" in *Ruddigore;* the joy and sorrow of "Brightly dawns our wedding day" in *The Mikado;* the pathos of "Strange adventure" in *The Yeomen of the Guard;* his melodies of simple, tender, beauty like "Prithee, pretty maiden" in *Patience*, "I know a youth" in *Ruddigore*, Strephon's first song "Good morrow, good mother" in *Iolanthe*, "The sun whose rays" in *The Mikado* (though there is an amusing vanity in its words), "When maiden loves" which Phoebe sings in *The Yeomen* as she sits at her spinning wheel, and the duet "I have a song to sing, O !", "Kind sir, you cannot have the heart" in *The Gondoliers*, the opening chorus of girls in the Second Act of *The Mikado* and the first chorus in *The Gondoliers*, "List and learn, ye dainty roses". I have mentioned various Gilbert and Sullivan operas here, but my own view is that the greatest of them are *Iolanthe*, *The Mikado* and *The Gondoliers*. The nearest approaches to this level in the world of light opera among their successors are André Messager's charming and romantic *Véronique* and *Monsieur Beaucaire;* yet neither they nor the works of any of Sullivan's contemporaries or predecessors in this field equalled his wide range of feeling, which was combined with musical humour and an exceptional gift for delicate orchestration.

One of the greatest of operatic comedies came towards the end of the nineteenth century and of Verdi's long life—virtually his only comic opera, *Falstaff*, in which he and his librettist Boito transformed Shakespeare's *The Merry Wives of Windsor*, by making certain alterations of the incidents and of the characters, and embodying some features from *Henry IV*, and above all by means of the witty and enchanting score. Falstaff's "honour" speech, by a happy touch, is accompanied by trills and grunts on the woodwind and double-basses; his soliloquy outside the "Garter" Inn at the beginning of the Third Act finishes with a wonderful orchestral trill starting softly and growing in volume to illustrate the increasing effect of the wine upon him. Together with these and many other humorous passages, we have Ford's moving monologue on jealousy, the beautiful, tender love music of Fenton and Nanetta, the exquisite music for the "fairies" in the last scene, and the rich good-humour of the final fugue. *Falstaff* is indeed a great comic opera, all the greater because it combines fun with so many other human qualities.

Most critics would probably hesitate to call Humperdinck's *Hansel and Gretel* a great operatic comedy; admittedly, it is the work of a *petit-maître;* but it is a fairy-tale opera for children, and through the freshness and charm of its melodies and its euphonious orchestration it has maintained its popularity for successive generations in many countries at Christmas time ever since its production in December 1893. Within its own genre it is a miniature masterpiece.

Rimsky-Korsakov's *Le Coq d' Or* (1909) is also a fairy story, fantastic, satirical, and, maybe, symbolical—of who knows what? Is it a comedy at all? Both King Dodon's sons are killed in battle, and in the last Act he kills the Astrologer, the golden cockerel comes to life and slays him with a peck, amid the laments of the people; but in the epilogue, the resurrected Astrologer tells us that the whole thing is a fairy tale and that only he himself and the Queen of Shemakha were human. The score contains some beautiful melodies, fascinating rhythms and richly coloured orchestration. It possesses an attractive, yet hard, brilliance, which seems to fit the strange tale and to place the opera on the borderline of greatness.

Many people would include Richard Strauss's *Der Rosenkavalier* among the great ones. They find much of its music entrancingly, ravishingly beautiful. They love its waltzes and do not feel their incompleteness as melodies to be unsuitable to the nature of the waltz. Ernest Newman[3] wrote that the closing scene of Act I, "has few equals in opera for the beauty and depth of its humanism", and called the trio for women's voices in Act III "magnificent . . . the emotional climax of the opera". Neville Cardus[4] described the work as "the best of all entertainments presented for the delectation of civilized men and women of all ages who go to opera". There is no denying the skill of it all, the wizardry of its instrumentation, or its interest from the standpoint of musical development, in that here for the first time in the history of opera, by discarding the old formal shape of the dance tunes, waltz music is woven into a continuous web of sound. Yet I confess that I find the emotion superficial, and the sophistication irritating. There are so many who sympathize with me in this, and who go further in their dislike of a work which objective, rather than subjective, criticism prompts me to place among the great operatic comedies, though a long way below those, for instance, of Mozart, Wagner and Verdi.

A much more light-hearted, less elaborate, and—I feel—more genuine and amusing affair is Weinberger's *Schwanda the*

[3] *Opera Nights*, pp. 522, 538. [4] *Ten Composers*, p. 90.

Bagpiper (1927), with its bewitching polka and other Czech dance melodies and its musical interpretation of a story combining fantasy, wit and romance; but perhaps it should be included among the great *light* operas of the nineteenth and twentieth centuries.

The score of Britten's *Albert Herring* is full of deft, descriptive, subtle touches, and the voice parts are sometimes lyrical in quality; but the libretto, based by Eric Crozier on a short story by Guy de Maupassant, is somewhat thin and long-drawn-out, and perhaps that is why the composer's talent does not seem to respond to it fully: the music is often interesting, rather than gripping or appealing. The central figure, as in *Peter Grimes*, is a feeble creature, not sufficient to carry the weight of the opera—even though here it is a comic opera—on his shoulders. And so—in spite of this work and *Let's make an Opera*—I had come to think of Britten as a composer mainly of tragic works so far as the stage is concerned, until the appearance of *A Midsummer Night's Dream*, which in my view surpasses all his previous operatic achievements. The composer and Peter Pears, who together wrote the libretto, show the same kind of ingenuity in it as Boito did in the case of Verdi's *Otello* and *Falstaff*. They make many cuts, transpose scenes, portions of scenes, and lines, and they omit most of the first part of Shakespeare's opening scene with Theseus, Hippolyta and Egeus—doubtless believing that the reference in their First Act to "the sharp Athenian law" compelling Hermia to marry Demetrius (and to "the peril of the Athenian law" in their last Act) and Theseus's eventual "o'erbearing" of her father's will, would be enough to take its place in the minds of the audience. As Theseus and Hippolyta do not appear until the final scene, the main action of the opera is divided between the fairies, the lovers, and the rustics—with the fairies predominating in potency. The authors of a work of art which is based on a previous one are fully justified in adapting it as they please, provided that they acknowledge their debt to it and that the result is a convincing and integrated creation in its own right. The fact that in this opera the fairies are the most important people does not mean that it is inferior in construction to its great original. In opera, simplicity of design in the libretto is an advantage, because music anyhow involves an enormous addition to the total ingredients. Wagner was not a great poet, but the dramatic structure of *Tristan* is perfect for a tragic music-drama, largely because Wagner eliminated so many of the legendary elements of the story in order to simplify it and thus to make it more suitable for his operatic purposes. Britten and Pears have similarly simplified Shakespeare's "lay-out" and have successfully transformed his perfect comedy with fairies into a perfect libretto apt for continuous music.

We find ourselves at once in the fairy wood, whose depth and mystery and dreamlike quality are reflected in the deep, soft, sliding notes of strings with which the opera opens. Britten has throughout caught the spirit of Shakespeare's bewitching play in terms of his own musical idiom. The orchestral score is delicate, subtle and magical. Each of the three main groups of characters is conceived in distant musical language. The fairies sing, for instance, with haunting celesta and woodwind effects, except Puck, who has a speaking, acrobatic rôle accompanied by trumpet notes; the only flaw here, I feel, is that Oberon is cast as a counter-tenor—no doubt consistently with the boy trebles of the other fairies and Tytania's soprano; but a light tenor voice would have been even better: I admit, however, that, like many others, I do not appreciate the effect of a counter-tenor's voice, and so this may be a purely personal, subjective reaction. To the lovers is allotted one lengthy theme, infinitely varied so that their music is in turns deeply pathetic, bewildered, wrathful and idyllic—but not more so than Shakespeare's words. The rustics are triumphantly and wittily portrayed in grotesque rhythms and intervals. The whole work is enchanting: and it shows that Britten is not only capable of conveying human moods, emotions, thoughts, religious feeling, and supernatural characters, but also the world of fairyland. This is a great fairy opera, composed in a century in which, for the most part operatic comedy had not advanced beyond the borderland of greatness.

CHAPTER 14

Shakespeare's Influence on Berlioz

BERLIOZ HAD THREE idols—Vergil, Shakespeare and Beethoven. I name them in their chronological sequence, not as indicating the order of importance in their effect on him. It would be unprofitable, even if it were possible, to compare his adoration of Beethoven with his worship of Shakespeare; it was natural that Berlioz, being what he was, should idolize at least one supremely great musician; but he was more intensely literary than most composers, and among the geniuses of literature even Vergil's influence upon him only manifested itself in one of Berlioz's compositions, albeit one of his greatest—the tremendous pair of operas which constitute *Les Troyens*. Shakespeare, on the other hand, pervaded Berlioz's life and art from his youth onwards. Many other composers have come under the Shakespearean spell. Verdi, above all, created three Shakespearean operas: but even those three were a far smaller proportion of his enormous total output than was the case with Berlioz; and we cannot say of Verdi, as we can of Berlioz, that Shakespeare's works were his Bible. Jacques Barzun[1] records that Berlioz's favourite plays were *Romeo and Juliet*, *Hamlet*, *King Lear*, *Macbeth* and *Othello*, but that he was also fond of *King Henry IV*, *Coriolanus*, *The Merchant of Venice*, *A Midsummer Night's Dream*, *Troilus and Cressida*, *Much Ado About Nothing* and *The Tempest;* and that in his writings, excluding scores and essays not reprinted, he alludes to or quotes about one hundred and fifty passages from twenty-two of the plays.

The story begins on the 11th September 1827, when Berlioz was exactly twenty-three and three-quarters. In his Memoirs[2]

[1] *Berlioz and the Romantic Century*, vol. II, p. 220, n.

[2] *Memoirs of Hector Berlioz* translated by Rachel (Scott Russell) Holmes and Eleanor Holmes; annotated, and the translation revised, by Ernest Newman, p. 66 f. In all subsequent references in this chapter,

he wrote: "I have now come to the grand drama of my life; but I shall not relate all its painful details. It is enough to say that an English company came over to the Odéon to perform Shakespeare's plays, then entirely unknown in France. I was present at the first performance of *Hamlet*, and there, in the part of Ophelia, I saw Miss Smithson, whom I married five years afterwards. I can only compare the effect produced by her wonderful talent, or rather her dramatic genius, on my imagination and heart, with the convulsion produced on my mind by the work of the great poet whom she interpreted. It is impossible to say more.

"This sudden and unexpected revelation of Shakespeare overwhelmed me. The lightning-flash of his genius revealed the whole heaven of art to me, illuminating its remotest depths in a single flash. I recognized the meaning of real grandeur, real beauty, and real dramatic truth, and I also realized the utter absurdity of the ideas circulated about Shakespeare in France by Voltaire:

Ce singe de génie
Chez l'homme, en mission, par le diable envoyé,

and the pitiful pettiness of our old poetic school, the offspring of pedagogues and 'Frères ignorantins'. I saw . . . I understood . . . I felt . . . that I had risen from the dead and that I must get up and walk."

"When[3] I left the theatre after seeing *Hamlet*, I was so shaken at what I had experienced that I determined never again to expose myself to the fire of Shakespeare's genius.

"The next day *Romeo and Juliet* was announced . . . I had a pass to the orchestra of the Odéon, but so afraid was I that the doorkeeper might have had orders to suspend the free-list, that the moment I saw the advertisement I rushed off to the ticket office to buy a stall and secure a seat at any cost. From that moment my fate was sealed. After the melancholy, the harrowing sufferings, the tearful love, the bitter irony, the black

---

Memoirs means that edition. I am grateful to the publishers, Messrs. Alfred A. Knopf, Inc. and to the late Mr. Newman for their assent to the quotation of these extracts.

[3] ibid., p. 68f.

meditations, the heartrending sorrows, the madness, the tears, mourning, catastrophes, and malign fortune of Hamlet—the dark clouds and icy winds of Denmark—the change was too great to the hot sunshine and balmy nights of Italy—to the love, quick as thought, burning as lava, imperious, irresistible, illimitably pure and beautiful as the smile of an angel; the raging revenges, delirious embraces, and desperate struggles between love and death. And so, at the end of the third act, scarcely able to breathe, stifled with a feeling as though an iron hand held my heart in its grip, I cried out, 'Ah, I am lost!' I must add that I did not then know a syllable of English, that I only dimly discerned Shakespeare through the misty medium of Letourneur's translation, and had no conception of the exquisite poetry in which his wonderful creations were clothed. Nor indeed am I much better off even now. It is far more difficult for a Frenchman to sound the deeps of Shakespeare's style than it is for an Englishman to appreciate the subtlety and originality of Molière or La Fontaine. Our two poets are rich continents, Shakespeare is an entire world. But the play of the actors, and especially of the actress, the succession of scenes, the action, and the tones of voice, penetrated me with the Shakespearean ideas and passions as the poor, pale translation never could have done. It was stated last winter in an article in the *Illustrated London News*, that after seeing Miss Smithson as Juliet I cried out, 'I will marry that woman! and I will write my greatest symphony on that play! I did both; but I never said anything of the kind. My biographer has endowed me with a vaster ambition than I possessed. This narrative will show what strange circumstances brought about a result which I was too completely overwhelmed even to dream of at the time. . . .

". . . After these two performances of *Hamlet* and *Romeo* I had no difficulty in keeping away from the English theatre; more experiences of that kind would have killed me; I shrank from them as one shrinks from physical pain; and the mere thought of exposing myself to such a trial made me shudder."

Some months later, we encounter Harriet Smithson and Shakespeare once more. Berlioz had avoided seeing her play Juliet or Ophelia again, but when he found that she was to appear in two acts of *Romeo and Juliet* at Huet's benefit at the Opéra-Comique, he resolved that his name should figure next to hers on the playbill, hoping thus to attract her attention. So he arranged for one of his overtures to be played. "When I went to the theatre for my rehearsal the English actors were finishing theirs; I came in just as the poor distracted Romeo carries Juliet off in his arms. As my eyes fell on the Shakespearean group I gave a loud cry and rushed out of the theatre, wildly wringing my hands. Juliet had seen and heard me . . . I had frightened her, and she asked the actors who were with her to watch me, *as she did not like the look of my eyes*."[4] Berlioz tells us that no words can describe what he suffered when Harriet left for Amsterdam the next day; he then proceeds to do so! "Even Shakespeare has never painted the horrible gnawing at the heart, the sense of utter desolation, the worthlessness of life, the torture of one's throbbing pulses, and the wild confusion of one's mind, the disgust of life, and the impossibility of suicide. The great poet has done no more, in *Hamlet*, than to count such suffering as among the most terrible evils of life.

"I had left off composing; my mind was paralysed as my passion grew. I could only—suffer."[5]

The marriage to Harriet Smithson proved unhappy; ultimately it broke down; but the spiritual and mental bond between Berlioz and Shakespeare lasted until the French composer's death.

In 1828–9 Berlioz's mind was steeped in Goethe's poetry, after reading Gérard de Nerval's new translation of the first part of *Faust;* but even when under that influence he composed his *Eight scenes from Faust*, Shakespeare was not absent from his thoughts and he introduced quotations from *Hamlet* or *Romeo and Juliet* at the beginning of each number of the score, in the original English words.

Except for the "Tempest" fantasia, which, though produced in 1830, was used afterwards, with slight alterations, as a Finale for *Lélio* and is discussed below, Berlioz's first composition on a Shakespearean subject was the overture *King Lear*. He had read the play in his turmoil of mind amid the hills near Florence

[4] *Memoirs*, p. 92. [5] ibid., p. 93.

in 1831 while waiting for news from Paris about Camille Moke, to whom he was then engaged; when he heard that she was to marry another, he was at first so overcome with jealousy that he conceived the idea of murdering her and her mother and his rival and then committing suicide; Tovey[6] even suggests that he might more suitably have called his overture "Othello"; but in fact he composed it during a month's subsequent stay at Nice, where the loveliness of the scenery brought balm to his troubled spirit: "I write the overture to *King Lear*. I sing. I believe in a God. Convalescence!"[7] Many writers have pointed out the impossibility of tracing the story of the play in Berlioz's music. He himself quotes the words of the King of Hanover: "Magnificent, M. Berlioz, magnificent; your orchestra speaks, you have no need of words. I have followed each scene: the entrance of the king into the council-chamber, the storm on the heath, the terrible prison scenes, and the laments of Cordelia. Oh! that Cordelia! how you have painted her! so tender and so timid! it is heartrending, and how beautiful!"[8] The composer does not, however, indicate in any way whether this interpretation accorded with his ideas in creating the work. The explanation, I believe, is that the overture was intended to be a portrait only of King Lear himself, with his impulsiveness, his outbursts of fury, alternating with tenderness and gentleness (represented by the lovely second subject on the oboe)—a figure of tragic grandeur, touched with pathos. After all, if Berlioz was, as Tovey suggests, talking nonsense in calling the work *King Lear*, it would be the only instance among his descriptive compositions in which he has done so. He knew what he meant, and he adored Shakespeare. The music fits the character of the king; Berlioz knew that he could not describe the whole play in one short overture; when he wanted to do that, for instance with *Romeo and Juliet*, he wrote a two-hour "dramatic symphony" for the purpose.

Lélio, ou le Retour à la vie is a "mélologue" cast in the form of six movements introduced by six soliloquies spoken by a musician called Lélio, and four of these (nos. 2, 3, 5 and 6) are associated with Shakespeare: in the first of them (no. 2) the

[6] *Essays in Musical Analysis*, vol. IV, p. 84.
[7] *Memoirs*, p. 130. [8] ibid., p. 479.

artist relates his thoughts about death to Hamlet's doubts and suggests that the Ghost's revelation of the murder might be the subject of a musical composition "full of a grand and sombre character": the "Chorus of Shades", which follows, carries out this idea. In another monologue (no. 3) Lélio speaks eloquently of the greatness of Shakespeare. In the fifth soliloquy (preceding "La Harpe Éolienne") his heart longs for a Juliet, an Ophelia. And in a later version of the work Berlioz prefaces the "Tempest" Finale with an adaptation of Hamlet's speech to the players, applied to musicians instead of actors. The "Tempest" fantasy, for chorus, orchestra and piano for four hands, suggests in its Prologue the atmosphere of Shakespeare's enchanted isle, and then (according to Berlioz himself) the Storm, the Action (disturbed in character) and the Dénouement, with its happy ending.

Berlioz had heard Bellini's opera on the subject of Romeo and Juliet, *I Montecchi ed i Capuletti*, in Florence in 1831, but was bitterly disappointed at Felix Romani's libretto, which "boiled down Shakespeare's masterpiece into . . . a bald book",[9] though he was "completely carried away" by the composer's treatment of "one of the principal situations". Eight years later he hit upon his own idea for the embodiment of the theme in "a symphony with choruses, vocal solos and choral recitatives".[10] His "dramatic symphony" in eight movements is usually performed in extracts, but it should be given complete, for it is a beautifully constructed, symmetrical whole. Because it is a symphony, it begins with an instrumental "Introduction", in the shape of a fine fugue in B minor, representing the strife and tumult in which the opening of the drama is set, but interrupted by a passage for trombones and ophicleide "with the character of a recitative" to mark the intervention of the Prince. In the "Prologue", which follows, soloists and chorus join with the orchestra in telling us—just as Shakespeare's Prologue does—of the feud of the two households, the lives and deaths of the "pair of star-cross'd lovers" and the final reconciliation of Capulet and Montague; but in Berlioz there is also an exquisite anticipation of the magic of Queen Mab; the chief musical themes of the work are foreshadowed; and thus we are

[9] *Memoirs*, p. 134f. [10] ibid., p. 230.

prepared both for the drama and the music that are to ensue.

In the third movement the orchestra symphonically depicts Romeo's rêverie and sadness, the brilliance of the ball in Capulet's Palace, and the background of conflict. After a distant "Goodnight" chorus sung by the young Capulets on their way home from the fête, we pass to the wondrously beautiful and eloquent love scene, in which Berlioz used only the instrumental idom, as being "by its very unliteralness infinitely more potent" (as he wrote in his Preface). This Adagio is succeeded by the "Queen Mab Scherzo": in the play, Mercutio tells Romeo how Queen Mab—

"gallops night by night
Through lovers' brains, and then they dream of love".

And as a scherzo for this dramatic symphony of love, Berlioz's vivid imagination was fired by the wizardry of Shakespeare's poetry in that speech[11] to conceive the most delicate fairy music ever created.

Juliet's funeral march for chorus and orchestra precedes the music of her death, just as in Shakespeare she is laid in the Capulets' monument when she is only thought to be dead. And in the next movement we are at the Tomb: Berlioz first returns to the turbulence of the Introduction; then at the end of the "Invocation" he faintly recalls the love theme; there is an allegro expressing the "delirious joy" of Juliet's awakening followed by the anguish and death of the lovers, with soft reminders of Romeo's rêverie and the love theme again. After this comes the Finale, with the anger and excitement of the assembling Montagues and Capulets, the conciliatory "Recitative and Air" of Friar Laurence and the gradual melting of hatred into love and friendship. Berlioz expected his audience to know Shakespeare's play; and provided that they do so, the significance of the music, even apart from the words sung by soloists and chorus, is clearly revealed.

In his *Memoirs*[12] (1845) Berlioz tells an amusing little story about his meeting with an Irishman in Vienna:—"a small man, with a clever, intelligent face, made his way to me through the crowd. It was the day after one of my concerts.

[11] Act I, Scene iv, 53–95. [12] *Memoirs*, p. 377.

" 'Sir,' he said briskly, 'you are French and I am Irish; so there is no national *amour-propre* in my opinion, and' (seizing my left hand) 'I beg your permission to grasp the hand that wrote the symphony of *Romeo*. You understand Shakespeare!'

" 'Certainly', I answered, 'but you are mistaken in the hand, as I always write with this one.'

"The Irishman smiled, took the right hand I offered him, pressed it very cordially, and went off, saying:

" 'Oh, these Frenchmen! these Frenchmen! They must laugh at everything and everybody; even at their own admirers.'

"I never knew the name of this kindly islander, who thus took my symphonies for left-handed children."

In describing a "marvellous" performance of the work which he conducted in St. Petersburg in 1847, Berlioz writes:—[13] "I do not know how often I was recalled. But I confess I did not pay much attention to the public; and such was the impression made on me by that divine Shakespearean poem as I sang it to myself that after the finale I fled for refuge into one of the side rooms, where Ernst found me a few moments later in floods of tears. 'Ah, your nerves are unstrung!' he said; 'I know well what that is'. And he supported my head and let me cry like a hysterical girl for a good quarter of an hour. Can you imagine a respectable tradesman of the Rue St. Denis, or the manager of the Opéra (in Paris, of course), witnessing such a crisis? Try to imagine what they would understand of the summer tempest in the artist's heart, its torrents and electric fires, vague memories of youth, first love, and Italian skies, blooming afresh beneath the burning rays of Shakespeare's genius; the apparition of Juliet, ever dreamt of, ever sought for, and never possessed; the revelation of the infinite in love and sorrow; my joy at having awakened some distant echoes of the voices of that heaven of poetry . . . then measure the roundness of their eyes and their gaping mouths . . . if you can! The first would say 'That gentleman must be ill, I will send him a glass of *eau sucrée*'; and the second, 'He is giving himself airs. I will have him put in the "Charivari".' "

His next Shakespearean pieces were composed in 1848 and

[13] ibid., p. 439f.

were two of the three works described (after Ovid) as "Tristia" (the other being the "Méditation Réligieuse"). The "Funeral March for the last scene of *Hamlet*", scored for orchestra, with soft notes for chorus, is prefaced by the final lines of the play uttered by Fortinbras, beginning—

> Let four captains
> Bear Hamlet, like a soldier, to the stage;

and is imbued with solemn, tragic grandeur. "The Death of Ophelia" is a pathetic ballad, written first for solo voice but afterwards transcribed for chorus and orchestra.

Harriet died in 1854. Berlioz, unable to attempt to give an idea of his grief, his pity for her past sorrows, his regret for their dead love, but filled with images of her as Ophelia and Juliet, invokes the spirit of the poet whom he idolized:—[14] "Shakespeare, Shakespeare! where art thou? He alone, of all intelligent beings, could have understood me . . . have understood us both. He alone could have looked with pity on two poor artists, at once loving and lacerating each other. Shakespeare, the true man, if he is still in existence, must know how to succour the wretched. He is our father, our father in heaven—if there be a heaven. An almighty being, wrapped in his infinite indifference, is an atrocious absurdity. Shakespeare alone is the good God to the soul of the artist. Receive us into thy bosom, O father, and hide us there. 'De profundis ad te clamo!' Death, annihilation, what are they? The immortality of genius—what? 'O fool, fool, fool! ' . . . Shakespeare! Shakespeare! Again I feel my sorrow overwhelming me like a flood, and again I seek thee:

'Father! father! where art thou?' "

Even in the one masterpiece of Berlioz that was inspired by his adoration of his other great idol in literature, Vergil, he turned to Shakespeare at a crucial moment. In Act V, Scene i, lines 9-12 of *The Merchant of Venice* Lorenzo says:—

> In such a night
> Stood Dido with a willow in her hand
> Upon the wild sea-banks, and waft her love
> To come again to Carthage.

[14] *Memoirs*, pp. 468–9.

And this evidently suggested to Berlioz that in choosing words for his love duet between Aeneas and Dido in *Les Troyens* he might adapt poetry from that exquisite scene between Lorenzo and Jessica beginning—

> The moon shines bright: in such a night as this

—that same scene which about eighty years afterwards gave birth to one of Vaughan Williams's loveliest works, the *Serenade to Music*. Both composers sensed the universal quality which is present in Shakespeare's lines even when separated from their context in the play. For this duet Berlioz conceived some of the most profoundly beautiful love music in the world.

From Vergilian tragedy with a touch of Shakespeare, Berlioz turned at the end of his creative career to Shakespearean comedy. He had suffered unhappiness and ill-health. *Béatrice et Bénédict* was, no doubt, an escape into an imaginary world of charm and fantasy. So eager, indeed, was he to escape that in framing his opera "imitated from" Shakespeare's *Much Ado About Nothing* he made Claudio and Hero into an ordinary pair of lovers, cut out the pathetic, nearly tragic, part of the story associated with them in the play, eliminated the evil figure of Don John, and concentrated his main action on Beatrice and Benedict; he also invented a new comic character, Somarone, a *maître de chapelle*. He employed spoken dialogue, much of it translated from Shakespeare, and wrote the simple and delightful verse of the musical portions himself.

After the gaiety of the overture, in which some of the music that follows is foreshadowed, the chorus, representing the people of Messina, sing triumphantly of the flight of the Moors from the siege of the town. They dance to an entrancing, lilting Sicilienne. Then comes Hero's air "Je vais le voir", with the limpid, tender beauty of its Largo, leading to a passionate "allegro con fuoco". The ensuing duet between Beatrice and Benedict embodies the wit and charm and liveliness of Shakespeare's portrayal of their characters. Then Don Pedro and Claudio join Benedict in a brilliant trio—with various changes of key and tempo—in which he protests and they chaff him at the prospect of his marrying. Now it is Somarone's turn—the "Épithalame grotesque" with choir and court musicians, to rehearse for the marriage of Claudio and Hero: he has cast it in the form of an engaging and humorous fugue, because (he says) "fugue" means "flight" and the two lovers are to think of the flight of time. Benedict's subsequent Rondo "Ah, je vais l'aimer" joyously expresses the sentiments contained in his words in the play "When I said I would die a bachelor I did not think I would live till I were married".[15] Berlioz's First Act ends with the exquisite duet between Hero and her maid Ursula as they wander in the garden in the serenity of evening.

The Entr'acte is largely a reprise of the Sicilienne, and Act II opens with the gay bustle of the "Improvisation" as Somarone and the chorus prepare for the wedding feast. Beatrice's recitative and air, beginning "Il m'en souvient", is a conflict of emotions, with alternations of time and mood. She, Hero and Ursula sing a charming trio, after which we hear the dulcet strains of the bridal chorus behind the scenes. There is a fine "Marche Nuptiale" sung by Beatrice, Ursula, Benedict, Don Pedro and chorus, with Claudio and Hero joining in later; a brief "Enseigne", "Ici l'on voit Bénédict—l'homme marié", for chorus, Don Pedro and Claudio; and finally, a "Scherzo-duettino" in which Beatrice and Benedict plight their troth and all the others join in happily.

Towards the end of his life, the romantic Berlioz renewed contact with Estelle, the love of his early youth—now an elderly lady, Madame Fornier. As long before as 1848 he had written a letter to her and signed himself "Despised Love"—which, as he said in a footnote to his Memoirs,[16] is an expression taken from Hamlet's most famous soliloquy. And he ended his *Memoirs* on 1st January 1865 by invoking her name—"Stella! Stella! I can now die without anger or bitterness"[17]—and quoting the closing lines of the marvellous speech which Shakespeare causes Macbeth to utter on hearing of the death of Lady Macbeth:—

> Life's but a walking shadow; a poor player,
> That struts and frets his hour upon the stage,
> And then is heard no more: it is a tale

[15] *Much Ado,* Act II, Scene iii, 263–4.
[16] *Memoirs,* p. 466.
[17] ibid., p. 531.

> Told by an idiot, full of sound and fury,
> Signifying nothing.[18]

The remaining few years of Berlioz's life until he died on 8th March 1869, were marked by sorrow and illness, but there is a grain of comfort in the way in which the town of Grenoble, albeit belatedly, fêted him with banquets and toasts only about six months before his death and in the fact that his last great work was an exquisite and happy opera on a subject taken from his adored Shakespeare.

Attempts have been made to compare the two creative artists—their rugged, uneven "Gothic" character, their vast imagination united to faults and even to lapses of taste. Such comparisons between artists working in different media need to be treated with great reserve; on close analysis, they usually turn out to be exaggerated or to amount to no more than a few points of resemblance. Berlioz, great though he was, did not approximate in artistic stature to Shakespeare. He professed himself an unbeliever, yet again and again he set sacred subjects to music; whereas Shakespeare, who, according to the bulk of the evidence, appears to have been a Christian, at any rate in the broad sense, only introduced religion occasionally into his works, though they are, of course, full of spiritual quality. Berlioz was a master of musical colour, which might perhaps be said to correspond to poetic imagery such as Shakespeare's. He was very wide in his portrayal of emotions, of scenes in nature, of fanciful and fantastic conceptions; but he was not myriad-minded like Shakespeare. It was natural that he should idolize the great English poet; but as an artist he did not resemble him very closely, and no other artistic creator has done so hitherto.

[18] *Macbeth,* Act V, Scene, v 24–8.

CHAPTER 15

Mendelssohn and the Problems of Shakespearean Production

A GOOD MANY years ago, James Agate stoutly maintained that Mendelssohn's music should always be used for productions of *A Midsummer Night's Dream*. More recently, Ronald Watkins, in his book *Moonlight at the Globe*, contended that the producer must set about exorcizing Mendelssohn. A compromise might seem impossible. Nevertheless I believe that the truth lies somewhere between these two extreme views.

Probably Agate would have been won over if he had witnessed Mr. Watkins's enchanting presentation of the play by the boys of Harrow School, where the Speech Room was converted internally into a model of the old Globe Theatre of Shakespeare's day.[1] On the other hand, Mr Watkins in his book, and the Headmaster in his foreword, claimed too much when they asserted that this is the only way.

I deny that Mendelssohn's overture—or any other part of his entrancing score—"conjures up a picture of gauze skirts, tinsel wings, and the block-toed shoes of a ballet-dancer." I have been present at performances of *A Midsummer Night's Dream* with Mendelssohn's music, but without such accompaniments as those. In any case, his music must be heard on its merits; and it creates marvellously the essential feeling of Shakespeare's fairies as portrayed in this particular play, the English countryside, the yokels, and the imaginary court; (it is, of course, a truism that though the scene is stated to be laid in Athens and a wood near it, the real atmosphere of the comedy is Elizabethan England). The bridal march may be associated in our

[1] Mr. Watkins has since produced many other Shakespeare plays there, on similar lines. Some of my remarks in this chapter apply equally to them.

minds with modern British weddings, but I cannot conceive anything less suitable for a church ceremony or more appropriate as a prelude to Shakespeare's Act V: like most great art, it is divine in character, but it is scarcely ecclesiastical.

I am speaking here of the intrinsic quality of the incidental music, which is as universal and immortal as Shakespeare's art itself, though not of so high an order of genius. It is at once romantic and skilful in craftsmanship, like Shakespeare, and it has the Shakespearean touch of fantasy. It is possible to be prejudiced against it because Mendelssohn was a foreigner and lived in the nineteenth century, but these facts are irrelevant if the actual character of the music fits the play. It is claimed that "it isn't Shakespeare". I maintain that it is, though I do not for one moment agree with Agate's insistence on its exclusive use for this play, and I thoroughly approve of and enjoyed the Harrow employment of Elizabethan madrigals and part-songs, though the words of them were not Shakespeare's.

Mendelssohn had a special taste and aptitude for fairy-like music: the rippling melodies and delicate orchestration of the overture and scherzo for *A Midsummer Night's Dream* perfectly embody the character of Shakespeare's fairies, but in the scherzos of the Octet and of the Scotch Symphony, the Finale of the violin concerto, and the so-called "Bee's Wedding" song without words, though he did not expressly associate them with fairyland, we get that same gossamer, fine-spun, rapid-moving delicacy which he showed in his score for the Shakespearean play.

The perpetual banishment of Mendelssohn's score from all stage performances of the play is unthinkable. If it is to be heard only in a concert room, it can never make its proper and intended effect when divorced from the play with which Mendelssohn meant it to be given. Or is it suggested that it ought not to be performed anywhere? If so, the same would apply to Sibelius's incidental music for *The Tempest;* and the countless lovely settings of Shakespearean poetry by Haydn, Dr. Arne, Schubert, Berlioz, Vaughan Williams, and Gerald Finzi (to name only a few), would have to be banished, because they were not contemporaneous with Shakespeare and were composed in idioms different from those of the music of

Shakespeare's day. The world of art would be very much the poorer, if this were done.

Many years ago, Granville Barker produced *A Midsummer Night's Dream* with music adapted from traditional English sources by Cecil Sharp. I wish that it could be revived. There is room for more than one form of incidental music for this or any other Shakespearean play, and more than one sort of production in other respects. It is not necessary to insist that only one method can be right, any more than that Toscanini's conception of Beethoven's Seventh Symphony is the only correct one, and that those of other conductors, in so far as they differ from his, are wrong. Shakespeare's art, like Beethoven's and that of other great creators, is wide enough to admit of more than one satisfactory mode of presentation.

In the case of those arts, such as music and drama, which are intended to be reproduced by performers, the original work as conceived by its creator, is somewhat like one of Plato's Ideas laid up in Heaven. It is a universal concept, of which the various performances are particular embodiments. These may differ from each other in detail, but so long as they do not play false to the essential character of the orginal, each of them in its way is a true reproduction of it. It is legitimate to object to them only in so far as they depart from its true nature.

Elizabethan music was entirely in keeping with the Harrow performance of *A Midsummer Night's Dream*, which sought to reproduce the other contemporary features. Mendelssohn would not have been suitable to it, but that does not mean that he cannot have his place in other productions of the play which may also be true to the essential character of Shakespeare, even though they employ more modern accessories.

The music is only one part of the problem which arises in putting Shakespeare on the stage. The vital ingredients in the proper presentation of one of his plays are that it should be uncut (apart from passages generally recognized as spurious), that it should be well cast and acted, and the language clearly and beautifully spoken. By these tests, many of the performances which I saw in my youth failed, but most of the far larger number which I have seen since the First World War have been satisfactory. All other factors (except one) are of less importance and it is in respect of these that the Harrow method differs from most of the other satisfactory post-1919 productions of my acquaintance.

The projection of the stage into the audience is like the old Globe, but it does not make so very much difference to the audience's appreciation of the play. So long as the actors are clearly audible and visible, it does not matter greatly whether they are on a modern type of stage or on a protruding platform. It is even possible that with the latter they might be difficult to hear when they have their backs to many of the audience, and if so, this disadvantage would more than offset the benefit of the alleged intimacy and of the feeling that in the soliloquies we are being taken into the speaker's confidence: we can feel this equally well when he comes to the front of a modern stage. Everyone likes the protruding platform at Harrow, but it is possible to exaggerate its importance. To compare the modern theatre to "gazing through the wrong end of a telescope" is an over-statement, and I find nothing "clogging" in a curtain or necessarily "banal" in a floodlight.

The use of much scenery for a Shakespeare play is not merely unnecessary, but a hindrance; but most recent producers have already reduced it to a minimum, recognizing that Shakespeare's words render the elaborate scenic effects of a previous generation out of place. Nor is it only at Harrow that Elizabethan costumes, or coloured dresses for the fairies in *A Midsummer Night's Dream,* have been used in modern times.

The one important respect in which the Harrow presentation differs from most other recent satisfactory productions is the casting of boys for the women's parts. Of course this had to be done for School performances, and the boys played them very well indeed. But simply because it was the practice three hundred and fifty years ago, it does not follow that its revival would be artistic or appropriate for a modern production in which adult professional actors are being employed for the men's parts. It is perfectly true that Shakespeare, being afflicted with the custom, made the best of it, by not having much passionate love-making on the stage as more recent authors have introduced. Nevertheless he portrayed women; and surely, once women were allowed to appear on the stage, they became the most natural people to act Shakespeare's women. Moreover, boy actors, however talented the producer, cannot be expected to possess the skill that a mature girl or woman, with her years of training and aptitude for the profession, has acquired. A boy instrumentalist could hardly be pitted against a fully developed professional musician. It is inconceivable that Shakespeare would not have welcomed good women actresses if he had been allowed them. And the fact that in a few (only) of his plays certain women in any case disguise themselves as boys, is a very minor point: there is no evidence that Shakespeare intended to play a kind of double joke by doing so—"boys pretending to be grown-ups behaving unconsciously like boys", as Mr. Watkins suggests—or that he even meant to produce a comic effect at all by this device: in fact, the internal evidence of the actual instances in question—Portia, Rosalind, Viola, Imogen—points the other way.

Nothing more delightful or more appropriate to Shakespeare could be imagined than that the plays should be produced in a modern replica of the old Globe, with protruding stage and so on, music by Shakespeare's contemporaries, and accomplished actresses matched by equally talented actors. But I see no reason why they should not also be presented, uncut and well cast, in theatres of modern type, with a minimum of scenery and with such incidental music as is required for the play, whether written by Shakespeare's contemporaries or by other composers, so long as it is true to the spirit of the drama and to the words and also does not drown the language as Alan Rawsthorne's clever music made Laurence Olivier's utterance of parts of King Lear's great storm speeches almost inaudible: why should the orchestra ever be caused to play while an actor is speaking?

A rigid adherence to every one of the practices prevalent in the days of the creator of a work of art is not necessarily the most artistic method, or even the most appropriate, in all respects, to the essential quality of his genius. In any case, there is room for other methods in addition. To hear Scarlatti played on a harpsichord conveys a better and truer impression of his works than if they be performed on a modern piano; but would anyone seriously contend that Bach's art is distorted when played on a pianoforte by performers who have a profound insight into his musical mentality, such as the late Harold Samuel, James Ching, Denis Matthews, or Rosalind Tureck? If it be not wrong to perform Parry's incidental music to *The Birds* of Aristophanes, as was done when that immortal comedy was so admirably produced in its original Greek at Cambridge a good many years ago, surely there is room for Mendelssohn in some performances of *A Midsummer Night's Dream.*

CHAPTER 16

Verdi and Shakespeare

BERLIOZ IDOLIZED SHAKESPEARE. That Verdi had a great love and veneration for him is shown by his having devoted three of his operas to Shakespearean subjects. We cannot, of course, measure the influence of a dramatic poet upon a composer by the mere number of such works, but in Verdi's case the striking feature is that the two operas of his which are generally regarded as the climax of his operatic career were inspired by Shakespeare, and that a third Shakespearean one had at least marked an early, but interesting, stage in his artistic development and even contained a few portions which were intrinsically worthy of their distinguished poetic origin.

Verdi's *Macbeth* was originally written in 1846–7 when he was in his early thirties; it was the tenth of his twenty-six operas; but he was an artist who developed gradually and reached the summit of his greatness in his seventies, and so it is not really surprising that, though it surpassed his earlier operas, he had not yet attained the quality which marks later works such as *Rigoletto, Il Trovatore* and *La Traviata*, much less the supreme mastery and genius of the two superb Shakespearean products of his old age, *Otello* and *Falstaff.* And if we contemplate it in relation to the great tragedy on which it is based, we are bound to be struck by its shortcomings. The comparison is really unfair; for the play is one of the supreme masterpieces of the greatest of all poetic dramatists written at the zenith of his career; whereas the opera is to a large extent the comparatively early work of a lesser genius. Hence it is quite natural for us to find that the general character of its music is immeasurably below that of Shakespeare's play in grandeur and beauty. In particular, the Three Weird Sisters of Shakespeare become in Verdi's hands a chorus of witches, whose music is of little interest or, at best, only pretty; there is a somewhat banal march associated with Duncan, and a rather feeble "toast" sung by Lady Macbeth in the banquet scene. On the other hand, much of her music is very striking, and Verdi's contribution to the sleep-walking scene is most impressive. The chorus and sextet at the end of Act I after Duncan's murder, and the orchestral music accompanying the apparition of the eight kings in the Witches' Cave and the fugue of the final battle, are very effective.

In 1850, Verdi contemplated an opera based on *King Lear* and returned to the idea in earnest three years' later, but it never materialized, and he was too busily occupied—also in 1850—to be able to set a libretto for a *Hamlet* opera.

In *Otello*, Verdi reached the summit of his powers. This does not imply that in my view it is a greater work than *Falstaff*—if indeed a comparison is possible between a tragedy and a comedy—but that in his case the top of the mountain, as it were, resembles less a single peak than a high plateau in which the masterpieces of his old age—both these operas and the *Four Sacred Pieces*—are in their various ways equally great. Boito provided him with a masterly libretto, in which, for their own particular operatic purposes, Shakespeare's first act was rightly omitted altogether, except for a passage in the love duet adapted most adroitly from Othello's speech to the Senate—

> She loved me for the dangers I had pass'd,
> And I loved her that she did pity them.

The killing of Emilia and the instruction for the torturing of Iago were eliminated, and in the opera there are certain additions to Shakespeare, of which the two most important are the "Credo" and Desdemona's prayer to the Virgin.

The "Credo" indicates the difference between Shakespeare's conception of Iago and that of Boito and Verdi. In the play, he is an entirely credible human being, an appalling villain actuated by jealousy of Othello and Cassio and by an overwhelming lust for power over his victims; Othello ultimately calls him "that demi-devil", but there is nothing supernatural about him; whereas in the opera, the "Credo" shows him to be an emissary of the Devil himself in human form: he believes in a cruel god who has created him in his own image, as the embodiment of evil, and man is the sport of the evil Fates. Verdi portrays this terrible creature in the most masterly fashion, with serpentine turns of insinuating melody and—in the "Credo"—a vast orchestral unison and a trill of terror.

Desdemona's prayer to the Virgin, accompanied by muted strings, is exquisitely soothing after the infinite pathos of the "Willow Song".

The music of *Otello* is such a powerful and moving counterpart of Boito's libretto that in its own Verdian, Italian, way it is as much a "music drama" as are the mature works of Wagner. There are in it no superfluous embellishments. It expresses in its own idiom all the passion, tenderness, evil subtlety, pathos, hatred, and ultimate remorse inherent in Shakespeare's tragedy. It is one of the greatest operas ever composed. If I say that nevertheless it falls below the play as a work of art, I hope not to be misunderstood. *Othello* is one of the tragedies which represent Shakespeare at the height of his powers—and Shakespeare was a greater genius than Verdi: there is not—even in *Otello*—that quality of grandeur, that sublimity of utterance which mark Shakespeare at his greatest. Verdi was simply incapable of rising to heights like those of Shakespeare's most tremendous poetry, such as is put into the mouth of Othello himself particularly. Among musicians, only Bach and Beethoven hitherto have done so, but their gifts lay mainly away from the stage, and the story of *Othello* would not have suited the creator of *Fidelio*. Wagner is, in the opinion of many, the greatest of all operatic composers, but so domestic a tragedy would not have appealed to his genius, with his addiction to legend and symbolism, so far as tragic themes were concerned. Verdi probably came as near to the Shakespearean *Othello* level as any composer hitherto could have done.

If *Otello*, for all its beauty and expressiveness, is surpassed by *Othello*, I believe that *Falstaff* is a greater work of art than the Shakespearean play on which it is based. A. C. Bradley[1], indeed, described the "parody" of the Falstaff of *Henry IV* in *The Merry Wives of Windsor* as "horrible", and said that "Falstaff was degraded by Shakespeare himself". But the best way to regard the matter, in my view, is to recognize that the fat knight of *The Merry Wives* is an entirely fresh character—merely a disreputable old man who becomes a butt for rough treatment. He may have been created in order to satisfy Queen Elizabeth's desire to see Sir John again and to see him "in love"; but he only resembles his namesake in his name and his girth. The play is a very entertaining farce, relying for its effect on situations rather than on character-drawing. But farce, I submit, is for that very reason inevitably a lower form of art than comedy. And so Verdi, in his brilliant and entrancing comic opera, had little difficulty in producing a greater work of art than the play which, however amusing, exhibits Shakespeare much below his best level both in its prose and in its poetry.

In the Verdi opera, with its splendid libretto by Boito, an element of the Falstaff of *Henry IV* is added to the picture by the incorporation of the speech decrying "honour", which Verdi set to the wittiest of music, with its trills and grunts on the wood-wind and double-basses. The description of Bardolph's red nose is also taken from that play, and Boito made various other alterations of *The Merry Wives*: for instance, Page, Slender, Evans and Shallow do not appear at all; Anne Page swops fathers and becomes Nanetta Ford, and Fenton, as her lover, only has Dr. Caius as a rival; and the disguising of Falstaff as an old woman is cut out. The music bubbles along with the utmost felicity, wit, subtlety, grace, and charm. Falstaff's soliloquy outside the "Garter" inn at the beginning of the Third Act culminates in a marvellous orchestral trill, which starts very softly and increases in volume to show vividly the growing effect of the wine on his system. But Verdi's music is not

[1] *Oxford Lectures on Poetry*: the lecture on "The Rejection of Falstaff".

"wholly" comic, as he himself described it to Monaldi (his future biographer). Ford's monologue about jealousy is very poignant; the love duet of Fenton and Nanetta and their other passages contain some of the most beautiful, tender love music ever composed. The music of the "fairies" in the last scene is full of delicacy and imagination; and the final fugue in which all the characters, including Falstaff, unite in treating the whole affair, indeed the whole world, as a big joke, is a rich climax of good-humour.

The earliest and latest of the three operas diverge in kind more widely than *Otello* from the plays on which they are based. Verdi's *Macbeth* differs from the play in its atmosphere and character. *Otello* does reflect (magnificently) the emotions and drama of *Othello*, even though it does not quite measure up to Shakespeare's immensely high poetic level in this tragedy and though its Iago is more specifically "diabolical" than Shakespeare's. *Falstaff* transmutes an amusing farce into a great comic opera.

CHAPTER 17

Shakespeare's "Henry VIII": Some Musical Analogies

IT USED TO be said that Shakespeare's *Henry VIII* is loose in structure, its characters inconsistent, its last act a mere appendage, and so on. But this idea has in recent years been contested, most convincingly, by G. Wilson Knight (in *The Crown of Life*) and by R. A. Foakes (Introduction to the 7th Arden Edition, 1957) who says (p. xlvii) that "structurally *Henry VIII* grows through a series of contrasts and oppositions". The play is, moreover, built on four trials—those of Buckingham, Katharine, Wolsey and Cranmer. Some light may be thrown on this architectural aspect if we compare it to certain musical structures.

The Ring consists of four operas, or one immense prologue and three huge music-dramas; yet it is also a unified work of art—or one music-drama in ten acts. Some characters—Wotan, Fricka, Erda, Alberich and Mime—after appearing in the *Rheingold*, recur in the later operas in varying degrees, whilst Fafner the giant reappears as a dragon, and Loge, who is prominent in person in the *Rheingold*, returns musically and scenically, being (as it were) embodied in the Magic Fire music of *Die Walküre*, *Siegfried* (Act III, Scene i) and *Götterdämmerung* (Siegfried's narrative in Act III); but we also find that though characters do thus overlap from one opera of the cycle to another, to a large extent fresh ones arise in successive operas or acts and become leading figures in the great story: Siegmund and Sieglinde disappear after *Die Walküre*, Brünnhilde appears in it and continues to the end of the cycle, but Siegfried is the leading male character in the last two operas; Wotan is seen no more after *Siegfried* Act III, scene i, and in *Götterdämmerung* the main figures apart from Siegfried and Brünnhilde are new to us—Hagen, Gunther and Gutrune. Yet no one suggests that *The Ring* is not a homogeneous whole; and if it be said that this is due to the "leitmotiv" system, the same might be said of *Henry VIII*, through which reverberate the great themes of justice and injustice, patience in suffering, salvation through self-knowledge and repentance, forgiveness, reconciliation and peace.

Henry VIII is rather like a cycle of plays in itself: there is unity in each of Shakespeare's two earlier, historical tetralogies—the first consisting of *Henry VI* Parts I, II and III, and *Richard III*, the second comprising *Richard II*, *Henry IV* Parts I and II and *Henry V*—in somewhat the same way as there was in Aeschylus's *Oresteian Trilogy* and doubtless in other cyclic tripartite dramas of ancient Athens which are lost to us. In all these cases, as in *The Ring*, characters recur or die or disappear and fresh ones arise and become prominent, and yet the unity of the whole is preserved. In *Henry VIII*, the trial and fall of Buckingham are followed by those of Katharine—which overlap with his, end after his death, and are succeeded by the fall of Wolsey. This in turn is followed by the trial of Cranmer, its happy issue on the intervention of the King, and his reconciliation with his enemies; and the play ends with the nation's joy in the birth of the young princess—a fitting conclusion to a play in which that baby's mother has played an important part and in which the real protagonist, perhaps, is the English people—rather in the same way as the Russian people, even more than Boris Godunov himself, is the leading character in Mussorgsky's opera.

Symphonies prior to Sibelius's Seventh were either in three or four movements; sometimes—in Haydn's and Mozart's, for instance—the movements, though contrasted, were felt to be spiritually or emotionally or intellectually in keeping with one another, though without any thematic link between them; in other cases, there might be an evident spiritual "story" inherent in the music, as in Beethoven's C minor, coupled with a certain thematic bond between movements (between the first and third movements there, and again between the third and fourth); or there might be, as in his "Pastoral", a unified "programme" which is not just fastened on to the music from outside but inherent and embodied in it and connects the movements into a consistent, artistic whole. In other symphonies, such as Franck's or Berlioz's "Fantastique" and *Harold in Italy*, or Tchaikovsky's Fourth and Fifth, or Elgar's two, the form is cyclic, with themes recurring significantly and in altered form in the different movements, and the unity of the work largely depends on the use of this kind of structure.

Sibelius, having adopted, broadly speaking, the type of these three- or four-movement works in his first six symphonies, decided in composing his Seventh to have a one-movement structure lasting about twenty minutes; but within that framework he embodied four sections which roughly correspond to the four movements of earlier symphonies, yet are connected together in a continuous web of sound and bound into a consistent whole.

The structure of *Henry VIII* somewhat resembles that of Sibelius's Seventh Symphony: instead of four separate plays forming a tetralogy, Shakespeare writes one play which contains four or five "dramas" within itself, but which is woven into a satisfying unity. It is, however, unlike that Symphony in that it achieves this result partly by means of its recurring "motives", like a Wagnerian music-drama, and partly through the personality of the King, who is a leading character throughout—progressing from his domination by Wolsey in the earlier parts of the play to his emergence as an instrument of true justice and benevolence in the latter part.

Henry VIII was Shakespeare's last play, and the Seventh was Sibelius's last symphony; true, Sibelius afterwards composed one of the greatest of tone poems, *Tapiola*, and his incidental music for *The Tempest;* but Shakespeare, correspondingly, was not only a dramatist: he first achieved fame with his "poems", and his wonderful sonnets were apparently created at different stages of his life. Nevertheless, we inevitably think of Shakespeare as *par excellence* a poet-dramatist and Sibelius as first and foremost a symphonist. The structural analogy between the last play of the one and the final symphony of the other is of course fortuitous but, I suggest, interesting.

CHAPTER 18

Great Love Duets

TO WRITE AT all comprehensively about the love of man and woman as expressed in music throughout the ages, would require an immense volume. So universal a theme naturally permeates the history of music as persistently as it does that of poetry, and is only less voluminous there than in poetry in so far as music itself reached its maturity at a much later stage than the other did. A book about love music would go back to folk song, and the old madrigals of Italy and England, and would have the whole range of German *lieder*, the "art songs" of other nations, and the wide world of opera as its material; cantatas would fall within its scope; and so, probably would many an instrumental movement, even though not verbally associated with a love story by the composer's express authority. To concentrate on love duets, however, at once limits the field to certain operas and a few other works, and I propose here to consider—not entirely in chronological order—some examples which seem to me to be either the greatest, or among the greatest, that the art of music has hitherto produced.

Gluck and Mozart were two of the supreme opera composers, but love duets do not figure much either in the only six operas of Gluck that count or in Mozart: either the story did not give opportunities for them, or the passionate emotions of man or woman were conveyed, not by both of them (except occasionally in recitative), but in arias sung by one or the other, or even by a character such as Cherubino, voicing the spell of love as a universal feature of humanity in the immortal strains of "Voi che sapete". Gluck's Orpheus and Eurydice sing no love duet (any more than they did in Monteverdi's opera); in *Armide*, the heroine and Rinaldo wait until the Fifth Act to do so, but what they sing is the seductive music of enchantment, appropriate to the alluring Armide, rather than that of the true devotion of young lovers. The fine duet between the two protagonists in the Third Act of *Paris and Helen* portrays the passion of Paris, but, on Helen's side, chiefly her sense of duty, as the wife of Menelaus, in opposition to it; their tiny love duet in Act IV is exquisite, but all too brief, and the one in the last Act is rather ornate in style; Gluck himself wrote in his dedication of the score that his subject was "a young lover, who stands in contrast with the strange humours of a proud and virtuous woman, and who, with all the art of ingenuous passion, ends by triumphing over her." It is the story of the illicit passion of a young man for a married woman, and hardly gave scope for a duet expressing fully romantic, mutual adoration, such as we find in the nineteenth century. And the only really great example of this that I can think of in Mozart is the duet between Belmonte and Constanze in Act III of *Die Entführung aus dem Serail*—a beautiful and masterly piece of virtuoso music; yet somehow the essence of true love is more convincingly portrayed by the utterly simple march music of flute, soft trombones and drums which accompanies Tamino and Pamina as they pass through the trials of fire and water towards the end of *Die Zauberflöte*, and the gentle strain which they sing ensemble between its two parts; even this short vocal passage is, however, no "love duet" in the ordinary sense: it tells of the serenity of two, who, faithful to each other, have passed through their ordeals, have learnt wisdom, and have finally attained happiness together.

Weber has sometimes been called the founder of the romantic school in music; but neither *Der Freischütz*, a fanciful tale of romantic love, nor *Oberon*, a fairy story, contains a love duet, though *Euryanthe* has a passionate one between the heroine and Adolar in the Second Act.

When Berlioz came to compose his "Dramatic Symphony", *Roméo et Juliette*, he cast the work midway in form between a cantata and a symphony; but though he employed voices, he unfolded the passion of the "star-cross'd" lovers, not through singers—as Gounod and Sutermeister did, or as most other composers and Berlioz himself, if he had been writing an opera, would probably have done—but by means of the orchestra, of which he was so consummate a master. This might seem to disqualify the "Scène d'Amour" from consideration here; Tchaikovsky, it might well be said, also portrayed the love of Romeo and Juliet in orchestral terms, yet we do not call the result a "love duet"; that is true, but in his "Fantasy Overture", that love is depicted simply by two beautiful themes in a single-movement work which also illustrates the other elements in the story—the quarrel between Montagues and Capulets, the character of Friar Laurence, the final tragedy, and so on. Berlioz's "Scène d'Amour", though it is itself a portion of a larger whole, is a distinct, and detachable, movement consisting entirely of a musical embodiment of Shakespeare's poetic duet—we might almost say, of the Balcony Scene; but Shakespeare was bound to make his lovers speak in turn, whereas Berlioz's Adagio expresses their mutual devotion—in all its depth, purity, and idyllic beauty: the opening melody on the muted violas seems to set the atmosphere—some have even suggested that the love song of the birds is depicted in it—and then the music of the two lovers enters softly and becomes more passionate and more richly coloured in orchestration until they have to part from one another.

In the Fourth Act of *The Trojans*, Berlioz, as it were, filled a gap left in Purcell's great little opera *Dido and Aeneas* (which contains no duet for the two lovers). It is a starlit night at Carthage, with the Mediterranean gently beating upon the shore.

In such a night
Stood Dido with a willow in her hand . . .

said Lorenzo to Jessica in the last Act of *The Merchant of Venice*.[1] We may think Jessica scarcely worthy of the exquisite poetry which Shakespeare made him pour into her ears in that scene; but love is there idealized, and Shakespeare inspired Berlioz both in the words and in the music which he created for this supremely beautiful love duet in his Vergilian opera. As Jacques Barzun says[2], "It is love made to seem infinite by association with the breadth of the physical universe"—a love so absorbing, so profound, so vast, that it seems to go even beyond the depth and idyllicism of the youthful passion of Romeo and Juliet depicted by Berlioz in his previous work. The duet is interrupted by Mercury, who strikes two blows on the shield of Aeneas hanging on a column and, crying "Italy" three times, recalls him to his mission. We have already known that their love was to end in tragedy, and, on Dido's side, in bitterness, and that she is to invoke curses upon him as she dies on the funeral pyre, even though these are to be submerged in the glory of the Trojan March and a prophetic vision of the Roman Capitol. But our knowledge of these coming events does not prevent our listening —entranced, uplifted—to the undying beauty of their love music while it is in progress.

There are many fine love duets in the earlier operas of Verdi, but I am content to concentrate on those in the two great Shakespearean works which crowned his achievements towards the end of his life. The long duet between the Moor and Desdemona at the end of the First Act of *Otello* begins softly with the tranquillity of love after the turmoil of victory over the Turkish fleet and the perils of the storm. For the present they can enjoy their happiness, and the kiss of rapture is portrayed by a

[1] *Merchant of Venice*, V. i. 9ff.
[2] *Berlioz and the Romantic Century*, vol. II, pp. 141–2.

passionate theme which is to recur on the orchestra with the utmost pathos at the end of the tragedy as Othello falls on Desdemona's dead body to words which recall Shakespeare's—

> I kissed thee ere I kill'd thee; no way but this,
> Killing myself, to die upon a kiss.

The contrast between this great love duet and the one between Fenton and Nanetta in *Falstaff* might be said to correspond to the antithesis in Wagner's case between the love music of Tristan and Isolde and that of Walther and Eva in *Die Meistersinger*. The young lovers in the Verdi comic opera voice their feelings in Act I, scene ii, most delicately in fragrant strains of tender devotion, which recur at other points of the score.

Considering that the love of Walther and Eva is one of the main elements in Wagner's opera, the amount of duet music between them is small in relation to the great length of the work. They sing an impassioned farewell to one another just before Magdalena escorts Eva away in the early part of the First Act, their music being based on the second of the love themes associated with Walther which had appeared in the Prelude, and on the motive which is eventually to form the final verse of the Prize Song. In the Second Act their love dialogue begins with a theme which had previously accompanied the scene between Eva and Sachs, but later it passes into a feverish orchestral development of the motive which in Act I had embodied the derision of the Masters—as Walther now imagines himself continually beset and tormented by them and urges her to escape with him; the Night-Watchman's horn is heard offstage, but Eva soothes Walther to the theme of the Magic of Midsummer eve. In the Third Act there is no love duet: the Quintet at the end of the first scene includes their love music, but this is combined with other strains reflecting the emotions of Hans Sachs, David and Magdalena; and in the closing scene the love of Walther is, as it were, consummated in his Prize Song and in the final homage to Sachs.

Love duets, as such, are more prominent in *The Ring* and *Tristan*. In *Die Walküre*, as soon as Siegmund staggers exhausted into Hunding's hut, the orchestra expresses Sieglinde's emotion in a tender motive of compassion, which is followed by a 'cello solo foreshadowing the great love duet that is to close the First Act. This duet really begins when she tells him of the sword which the mysterious stranger (Wotan) had struck into the ash tree and which only the mightiest of heroes should pluck forth. The sword motive, the spring song, and the love theme, transmuted into joyous rapture, are the main elements in the passionate and exultant music which streams from Siegmund, Sieglinde, and the orchestra until the curtain falls. In the Second Act, the scene between these two is filled with Sieglinde's agonized terror of Hunding, who is in pursuit of her, but on the orchestra there are, also, infinitely pathetic reminders of the love music of the previous Act.

The last scene of *Siegfried* consists mostly of the vast love duet between the hero and Brünnhilde. The orchestral music has died down to utter serenity, and Siegfried sees her sleeping form, which in its armour he takes to be that of a man; when he discovers that it is a woman, an "animato" motive voices the love and the fear which he experiences for the first time. Brünnhilde awakes and greets the world and her deliverer, and their rapturous ensemble begins. The melody in E major enters, which figures also in the "Siegfried Idyll"; it is the only tender strain in this long duet, which is mainly triumphant and heroic in character. And the "Sunrise Duet" in the First Act of *Götterdämmerung* is also as much heroic as passionate; this is the last great love duet in *The Ring*: for when Siegfried and Brünnhilde are again alone together on the rocky mountain-top, he is disguised as Gunther and their music takes on a deeply tragic, at times sinister, character, as the dark clouds of the tremendous drama gather round them.

From the loves of these semi-divine creatures in *The Ring* we can pass to the story of Tristan and Isolde, who in Wagner's opera (even though not in all the legendary versions of the subject) are completely human beings. The love interest in *Die Meistersinger* and *The Ring* is of immense importance; but in *Tristan* it overrides everything else—the devotion of Brangäne to Isolde, or Kurvenal to Tristan, the latter's loyalty to his uncle, King Marke, and the nobility of the King himself. The love of Tristan and Isolde had begun, as we learn from her narration in Act I, when her desire to kill him in revenge for his conquest of Morold, her betrothed, had yielded to compassion as they looked at one another when he lay wounded in her care. Tristan is now altruistically bringing her to Cornwall to be Marke's bride. That which they believe to be an elixir of death and the gateway to eternal love in the next world, turns out to be a love potion, which releases the restraints that have kept their love in check hitherto. It is the orchestra that first reveals the truth, with its memories of the love music from the opening of the Prelude and its crescendo of passionate outpouring; then, after a long silence, Tristan and Isolde are at last able to utter one another's names and to sing together in rapture, before the intervention of Brangäne and of Kurvenal and the arrival of the ship at Cornwall cause them to realize the tragic implications of their love.

The music which Wagner composed for them and for the orchestra in the long, wondrous scene in the Second Act when they are together, while Brangäne keeps watch on the tower, is no ordinary "love duet". It is, of course, true love music—of the most ecstatic, the most passionate, and, at the same time, the tenderest kind imaginable; but it is something more: it takes on a mystical cast, as they link their love with the thought of Death and Night—an eternal night of true love—in contrast with this deceitful world of Day in which we live our normal lives. The beautiful love themes follow one another in succession, each undergoing subtle changes and intertwining their phrases together—until the crash comes with the entry of Marke, Melot and the courtiers, and the lovers' blissful dream is harshly shattered.

All these great examples that we have been considering are the music of lovers who have not, or have not yet, entered on marriage, except one—the duet between Otello and Desdemona: this is happy while it lasts, but we who know the story cannot avoid being conscious of its tragic sequel; and if we have already heard the opera we are aware of the poignant treatment of one of its main themes which Verdi is to introduce at the end of the work. The one supreme operatic expression of wedded love with a happy ending is the duet in the Dungeon scene in Beethoven's *Fidelio*, "O namen-namenlose Freude", composed by a man with so difficult a nature that it was fortunate—certainly for the various women with whom he fell in love, and probably for himself too—that he remained a bachelor all his life. Leonora, disguised as a man, and aided by the arrival of the Minister, Don Fernando, which has been signalled by the trumpet call outside, has rescued her husband, Florestan, from death at the hands of Pizarro in the nick of time, and together they sing this song of exalted, unqualified joy, love, and gratitude to God.

PART IV

HOW MUSIC CAN INFLUENCE A POET

CHAPTER 19

Robert Browning, The Poet Musician: (1) Biographical

MUSIC HAS CONSTANTLY been fertilized by literature in various ways in the course of its history. But—changing the metaphor—the traffic has not all been in one direction. Literature has also been enriched by music. Many distinguished men of letters, it is true, have been unmusical, and some people have even had a good deal of fun from the mistakes made by eminent novelists and others in their references to music and musicians. But among our greatest English poets, Shakespeare, Milton and Browning have all shown themselves to have a special love for the sister art. At least two books have been devoted entirely to the subject of music in Shakespeare, and in *The Shakespearean Tempest* Professor G. Wilson Knight demonstrated how "tempest" and "music" are the central symbols in his works—"tempest" meaning both storms in nature and the turmoil of discord in men's souls, whilst music is associated with still airs and waters and sweet flowers, with love and peace and good news and "all that is most divine and etherial". Milton's poetry contains much internal evidence of his love of music. But in Browning's case the matter is more specific: for he wrote several great poems actually dealing with musical subjects, in addition to introducing the theme of music into other poems in various degrees and also making incidental allusions to it.

Let us first look at the biographical side. Browning's mother was the daughter of William Wiedemann, a German who had settled in Dundee and married a Scotswoman, and it was through her that he inherited his passion for music. Wiedemann had been an accomplished draughtsman and musician,[1] and she herself loved to sit at the piano in the evening. As a child,

[1] Mrs. Sutherland Orr: *Life and Letters of Robert Browning*, p. 26.

Robert crept downstairs from bed to listen, and, when she ceased to touch the keyboard, flung himself into her arms, whispering, amid sobs, "Play, Play".[2] One of his earliest memories was of her playing Avison's once popular Grand March in C major, which

> timed in Georgian years
> The step precise of British Grenadiers.

He was taught at home by tutors, and his training included music, singing, dancing, riding, boxing, and fencing. Abel, a pupil of Moscheles, was his instructor in pianoforte technique. John Relfe, musician in ordinary to the King, was the son of a former organist at Greenhill Hospital, was himself reputed to be one of the best teachers of the pianoforte in London, and was a composer and author of a valuable treatise on counterpoint: Robert was one of his pupils in musical theory.

From fourteen to sixteen, Browning tended to think that musical composition might prove to be his *métier*. He wrote some settings of songs, which he himself sang—e.g., Donne's "Go and catch a falling star", Hood's "I will not have the mad clitie", and Peacock's "The mountain sheep are sweeter"; but he afterwards destroyed all of them. In his later teens, his chief companions were his cousins, James, John and George Silverthorne, all of whom were musical. As a boy, he had conceived a "calf-love", which developed into a warm friendship, for Eliza Flower, who appears to have been a talented composer. In 1842 he wrote asking her to set the lyrics of his "Pippa Passes" to music, and in 1845 he wrote to her about a coming concert of her sacred compositions, saying how greatly he admired her art; but she was, then, slowly dying of tuberculosis.

Mrs. Bridell-Fox described her first meeting with him, when he was twenty-three or twenty-four: "I remember . . . when Mr. Browning entered the drawing room, with a quick, light, step; and on hearing from me that my father was out, and in fact that nobody was at home but myself, he said: 'It's my birthday; I'll wait till they come in', and sitting down to the piano, he added: 'If it won't disturb you, I'll play till they do.' And as he

[2] W. Hall Griffin and H. C. Minchin: *The Life of Robert Browning*, third (1938) edition, pp. 15–17.

turned to the instrument, the bells of some neighbouring church suddenly burst out with a frantic, merry peal. It sounded, to my childish fancy, as if in response to the remark that it was his birthday." What would we not give to know what he played, or intended to play, on the piano on that occasion! But—as a clue to his musical tastes in pianoforte music in his bachelor days—W. Hall Griffin and H. C. Minchin's book[3] records that he loved to play Beethoven or Handel on the pianoforte in the drawing room at the Hatcham house where he lived with his parents.

Browning's letters to Elizabeth Barrett before their marriage contain various musical allusions. On 1st March 1845 he wrote "I seem to find of a sudden—surely I knew before—anyhow, I *do* find now that with the octaves on octaves of quite new golden strings you enlarged the compass of my life's harp with, there is added, too, such a tragic chord, that which you touched, so gently, in the beginning of your letter I got this morning". (Elizabeth, in her reply protested "But I did not mean to strike a 'tragic chord'; indeed I did not!")

On 13th May 1845 Browning wrote "I am nearly well—all save one little wheel in my head that keeps on its sostenuto" (and he quotes, in music type, a B-flat minim over the top line of the bass clef).

In his letter of 14th June 1845 he speaks, as he so often does, of his poetry as "music", and Elizabeth replies in similar language.

After this, he becomes, at times, more specific in his references to music. We get further evidence of his love of Beethoven's art in his letter of 15th August 1845: "I remember, in the first season of German opera here, when *Fidelio's* effects were going, going up to the gallery in order to get the best of the last chorus —get its oneness which you do—and, while perched there an inch under the ceiling, I was amused with the enormous enthusiasm of an elderly German," and next week, he says, he (and his cousin) "went again to the Opera and again mounted at the proper time" and again were intrigued by the excited gestures of the same German "as the glory was at its full".

On 11th September 1845, he wrote, "So, wish by wish, one

[3] op. cit., p. 123.

gets one's wishes—at least I do—for one instance you will go to Italy.

And on 3rd March 1846, he wrote "And the rest shall answer *yours*—dear! Not much to answer. And Beethoven, and Painting, and—what *is* the rest and shall be answered."

His letter to her of 7th March 1846, contains the longest passage about music in their mutual correspondence: "For music, I made myself melancholy just now with some 'Concertos for the Harpsichord by Mr. Handel'—brought home by my father the day before yesterday; what were light, modern things once! Now I read not very long ago a French memoir of 'Claude le Jeune' called in his time the Prince of Musicians—no, 'Phoenix'—the unapproachable wonder to all time—that is, twenty years after his death about—and to this pamphlet was prefixed as motto this startling axiom—'In Music, the Beau Ideal changes every thirty years'—well, is not that *true*? The Idea, mind, changes—the general standard . . . so that it is no answer that a single air, such as many one knows, may strike as freshly as ever—they were *not* according to the Ideal of their own time—just now, they drop into the ready ear—next hundred years, who will be the Rossini? who is no longer the Rossini even I remember—his early overtures are as purely Rococo as Cimarosa's or more. The sounds remain, keep their character perhaps—the scale's proportioned notes affect the same, that is—the major third, or minor seventh—but the arrangement of these, the sequence of law—for them, if it *should* change every thirty years! To Corelli, nothing seemed so conclusive in Heaven or earth as this

I don't believe there is one of his sonatas wherein that formula does not do duty. In these things of Handel that seems replaced by—

that was the only true consummation. Then—to go over the hundred years—came Rossini's unanswerable coda:

which serves as base to the infinity of songs, gone, gone—*so* gone by! From all of which Ba[4] draws *this* 'conclusion' that these may be worse things than Bartoli's Tuscan to cover a page with!—yet, yet the pity of it! Le Jeune, the Phoenix, and Rossini who directed his letters to his mother as 'mother of the famous composer'—and Henry Lawes, and Dowland's Lute, ah me!"

Then on 15th May 1846, Browning gives another indication of the importance of Beethoven in his life:

"The more I need you the more I love you, Ba—and I need you *always* . . . all I mean to say is that at times when I could, I think, shut up Shelley, and turn aside from Beethoven, and look away from my noble Polidoro—my Ba's ring—not to say the hand—ah, you know, Ba, what they are to me!"

After their marriage on 12th September 1846, they did not need to correspond, as they were never parted until her death, but on 7th January 1847, Elizabeth wrote from Pisa to her sister Henrietta—

". . . As to the piano, I begin to despair. I was foolish enough to say that I did not play—and the idea of even *seeming to have*

[4] "Ba" was Elizabeth's nickname (derived from "baby") from her infancy.

anything himself . . . (though I have talked myself hoarse about my love of music and so on) is quite enough to make Robert turn back determinedly. He calls it a foolish expense, and won't listen to it—Such pleasure it would be to hear him—Mrs. Jameson told me his playing was 'full of science and feeling', which I can easily believe, for he could not do a thing moderately well."

However, Benét[5], in relation to October 1847, when they had settled in Florence, tells us "They had rented a grand piano for ten shillings a month, for Robert was not only familiar with the whole 'grammar of music' but also a most agreeable pianist". Elizabeth referred to the hire of the piano in her letter to Mrs. Martin of 24th April 1847, and also wrote "Robert played Shakespeare's favourite air 'The Light of Love' " (on Shakespeare's birthday, when Mrs. Jameson was with them that evening), and she mentions this in her letter to her sister Henrietta of about the same date.

G. W. Curtis, an American journalist, long afterwards recalled how in 1847 he had listened to Gregorian chants and a hymn by Pergolese, as Browning sat and played upon the organ of the monastery chapel at Pelago (thirteen miles along the valley of the Arno from Florence) upon which it was believed that Milton played two hundred years before.[6] And we read[7] how in the winter of 1847–8, when still in furnished rooms in Florence, "they read, made music, talked much and wrote a little".

When they were settled at the Casa Guidi, and when their son, Robert Wiedemann (nicknamed Penini, Peni, or Pen—"Penini" being his childish attempt to pronounce his second name—), was a small boy, Elizabeth wrote to Henrietta on 12th February 1855: "Penini has remarkable quickness; and we might, by a little *pushing*, make him do anything: but we won't push, be certain! Robert says if we pushed him in music for instance, he would make an 'infant wonder' of him in two years. We want instead an intellectual man, of healthy development. . . .

"Robert teaches him beautifully. I confess I thought the

[5] *From Robert and Elizabeth: a further selection of the Barrett-Browning family correspondence* (John Murray, 1936): introduction and notes by William Rose Benét; p. 85.

[6] Griffin and Minchin, op. cit., p. 161. [7] ibid., p. 162.

system rather dry for so young a child—all those scales! But Robert insisting that I should interfere as little with his music as he did in my departments, I was silent, and now confess him to have been right and justified in his resolution of well-grounding his pupil. I hear Penini answering questions I should be a little puzzled at myself. He is very *vif* and ardent about his music—anxious to get on—and of course the advantage is great of having such a teacher as Robert, who is learned in music and teaches nothing superficially. The child sits by the fire with a music book and reads the notes aloud, quite fast. It's funny to hear 'e, totchet, sharp', etc."[8]

On 3rd August 1856, when they were visiting London, she wrote from 39 Devonshire Place[9]: "One of the best evenings of all was at the Hallés (the great musical artist's) last Thursday in Bryanston Square. He played Beethoven divinely—and there were other artists there—for instance, Mrs. Sartoris who sang. The music was first rate altogether." (In a letter about their visit to Rome in the early months of 1854, quoted by Mrs. Sutherland Orr[10], she referred to the "excellent music" which they heard at Mrs. Sartoris's house once or twice a week.) She wrote to Ruskin from Rome on 1st January 1859, "His (Peni's) musical faculty is a decided thing, and he plays on the piano quite remarkably for his age (through his father's instruction) while I am writing this".

Mrs. Sutherland Orr[11] gives a charming description of the musical relationship between Robert and his son when the latter was a child:— "He (Penini) would extemporize short poems, singing them to his mother, who wrote them down as he sang. There is no less proof of his having possessed a talent for music, though it first naturally showed itself in the love of a cheerful noise. His father had once sat down to the piano, for a serious study of some piece, when the little boy appeared, with the evident intention of joining in the performance. Mr. Browning rose precipitately, and was about to leave the room. 'Oh!' exclaimed the hurt mother, 'you are going away, and he has

[8] E. B. B.: *Letters to her sister* (Henrietta) 1846–1859, edited by Leonard Huxley, LL.D., p. 211. [9] E. B. B.: *Letters to her sister*, op. cit. [10] op. cit., pp. 288ff. [11] op. cit., pp. 305f.

brought his three drums to accompany you upon.' She herself would undoubtedly have endured the mixed melody for a little time, though her husband did not think she seriously wished him to do so. But if he did not play the piano to the accompaniment of Pen's drums, he played piano duets with him as soon as the boy was old enough to take part in them; and devoted himself to his instruction in this, as in other and more important branches of knowledge."

(From these last seven words and Mrs. Sutherland Orr's repeated and tantalizing silence everywhere on the nature or identity of the music which was performed and in which Robert delighted, it is perhaps a fair inference that she herself was little interested in the art.)

Two other references to music in the period of Browning's life prior to Elizabeth's death in June 1861 may be cited here.

The first is in a letter from him to Frederic Leighton, written at Siena on 9th October 1859: "I shall slip some day into your studio, and buffet the piano, without having grown a stranger."

The other is an extract from an article by Wilfrid Meynell in the *Athenaeum*, 4th January 1890.[12] "When, in autumn, 1860, W. M. Rossetti called on the Brownings at Siena, in company with Vernon Lushington, whom Browning had not met previously, the talk fell on the compositions of Ferdinand Hiller, which Lushington commended. 'Ah, now I understand who you are,' said Browning. 'When I find a man who shares with me a liking for Hiller's music, I can see into him at once; he ceases to be a stranger.' 'I don't know whether you care for music, Mr. Browning', said a new acquaintance of later days—a young lady—'but if you do, my mother is having some on Monday.' 'Why, my dear,' he answered, perhaps half believing what he said, 'I care for nothing else'."[13]

After Elizabeth's death, Browning (with "Pen") returned in due course to London; he kept up a correspondence with their dear friend, Isabella Blagden, and in this[14] we find several interesting passages about music:

[12] Quoted by Griffin and Minchin, op. cit., p. 287.

[13] The latter part of this extract, of course, relates to an incident during Browning's widowhood.

[14] *Dearest Isa: Robert Browning's letters to Isabella Blagden.* Edited and with an introduction by Edward C. McAleer.

London, 19th May 1863 (concerning "Pen" and himself): "We go to Ella's concerts, and Hallé's, and though there is too little practising, his general taste and intelligence in music improve". (Professor John Ella [1802–88] was a violinist, musical editor of the *Athenaeum*, and founder of the Musical Union, which gave chamber concerts.)

Cambo près Bayonne, Basses-Pyrenées, 19th August 1864: "I know Hallé, Joachim, and others, and make them play at parties where I meet them—the last time I saw Hallé, at his own house, he played Beethoven's wonderful last Sonata—the Thirty-second—in which the very gates of Heaven seem opening."

London, 19th December 1864: "Pen . . . is so good and promising: I shall be increasingly nervous about his particular success at College—two years hence—because I have been trying an experiment, you see, in resolving to *broaden* his acquisitions, instead of deepen them in one or two respects, to the detriment of all the rest: there can be no doubt that, had I *cut* off the modern languages, drawing and music, he would even by this time be nearly fit for his particular work at Balliol: but I look further than the mere college career—and of course it will be a success indeed if I get deepness enough in Greek and Latin with the other acquisitions: but folks frighten me a little when they tell me, as two people, strangers to each other, did last week, that merely to enter Balliol—pass the matriculation—is equivalent to taking honours at another college: well, we're *in* for it: Pen grows increasingly considerate, at least, and approximately anxious—mathematics seem doing him good: and how can I regret that he plays Bach and Beethoven understandingly?—as he certainly does."

London, 19th July 1867: "A fortnight ago, I was talking about Rubinstein (he is a marvellous player, beyond what I remember of Liszt, and immeasurably superior to everybody else)—a lady said 'And now it is too late to hear him'. I said 'No—I know he will be playing at Erard's, quite alone, this afternoon'.—'Will you take me?' 'And me,' said one sister, 'and me' said a third. So we all started: I think Rubinstein was a little startled as they sailed in—the three loveliest women in

London, perhaps—one being incomparable. He played divinely."

London, 19th June 1868: "I heard Rubinstein play at a party whence I returned late" (the night before Arabel Barrett died).

London, 24th February 1870: "There is a good—charming indeed—little singing German lady, Miss Regan, who told me the other day that she was just about revisiting her aunt, Mad^{e}. Sabatier—whom you may know, or know of."

(Anna Regan [1841–1902], German singer, was known for her excellent renderings of Schubert's songs. In 1869 she went to London with her teacher, Mme Sabatier, and sang at the Philharmonic, Crystal Palace, Hallé's recitals, etc. Caroline (Unger) Sabatier [1805–77] was a famous contralto, who sang under Beethoven: she retired after her marriage [1840] to a Florentine gentleman.)

London, 22nd March 1870: "Yes, I have known Mad^{e}. Schwabe this many a day: good, impulsive, not wise at all, but generous abundantly. I dined with her last year and heard Rubinstein."

(Mme Julie Salis Schwabe, was a patron of music, a philanthropist, and the founder of a girls' school in Naples [1861]. Elizabeth Browning knew her in Paris and in 1860 in Rome, and Robert went to concerts at her home in London.)

On 10th March 1877, Browning sent a short, hasty letter to Mrs. Fitz-Gerald, of Shalstone Manor, Buckingham about Joachim's investiture with the Doctor's degree at Cambridge; he declared that this ceremony, the concert given by the great violinist, and his society, were "each and all" worth the trouble of the journey.[15]

Mrs. Sutherland Orr[16] tells us that in Venice, while staying at his son's house, Browning "assisted at one musical performance which strongly appealed to his historical and artistic susceptibilities: that of the *Barbiere* of Paisiello in the Rossini theatre and in the presence of Wagner, which took place in the autumn of 1880".

[15] Mrs. Sutherland Orr, op. cit., p. 452. [16] op. cit., p. 484.

In his letter to Mrs. Fitz-Gerald of 24th September 1881, from Venice, Robert tells of his and his sister's visit to "Les Charmettes", the house of Rousseau—kept much as when he left it: "I visited it with my wife perhaps twenty-five years ago, and played so much of 'Rousseau's Dream' as could be effected on his ancient harpsichord: this time I attempted the same feat, but only two notes or thereabouts out of the octave would answer the touch."[17]

The last reference to music in Browning's correspondence that I have discovered occurs in his letter of 21st October 1887 to the Rev. J. D. Williams, from his London abode: he writes that he has had two invitations to go to Cambridge for the Greek play—one from the Master of Trinity, the other from Stanford, the composer: "I provisionally accept the hospitality of the latter . . . I observe that the *Oedipus* is brought out under the auspices of Professor Kennedy . . . Mr. Stanford writes the music, which went very well in the case of the *Eumenides*".[18]

So much for the evidence of Browning's letters. It remains to record that during those years in London after his wife's death he used to go to practically every important concert of the season with an old friend, Miss Annie Egerton Smith. Mrs. Sutherland Orr states[19] that he always declared that from his indulgence of his passion for music he derived some of the most beneficent influences of his life; but that, after Miss Egerton Smith's sudden death in 1877—almost in his presence, at the villa "La Saisiaz", near Geneva—when she was no longer there to call for him in her carriage and act as his musical companion, the habit of concert going was broken. This authoress continues: "Time was also beginning to sap his strength, while society, and perhaps friendship, were making increasing claims upon it. It may have been for this same reason that music after a time seemed to pass out of his life altogether. Yet its almost sudden eclipse was striking in the case of one who had not only been so deeply susceptible to its emotional influence, so

[17] ibid., p. 482.
[18] Thurman L. Hood: *Letters of Robert Browning, collected by Thomas J. Wise.* [19] op. cit., p. 440.

conversant with its scientific construction and its multitudinous forms, but who was acknowledged as 'musical' by those who best know the subtle and complex meaning of that often misused term."

In saying that music "seemed to pass out of his life altogether", she is somewhat overstating the case. For it will be noted that a few of the musical incidents mentioned above occurred after Miss Egerton Smith's death. Moreover, Griffin and Minchin[20], after recalling Browning's lifelong love for music, his powers as an organist at Vallombrosa (in his maturity), his charming improvisations at the piano to the delight of his friends, his composition of songs, his friendships with Joachim and Clara Schumann, recount that "At Asolo, during the last months of his life, he would sit in the little loggia of his friend Mrs. Bronson, and in the gathering twilight would discourse old-time melodies upon the little tinkling spinet which his hostess had provided for his pleasure".

CHAPTER 20

Robert Browning, the Poet-Musician:

(2) Music in Browning's poetry

ALTHOUGH BROWNING WAS the most intensely musical of the great English poets, he was always, in his poems dealing with musical subjects, a poet first and secondly a musician or music lover. He drew from music meanings relating to life in general or to the universe or to religion: it had for him profound, far-reaching analogies or associations with humanity and with the non-musical world; and for his purpose it was not necessary to take the art of the greatest composers as his theme; indeed,

[20] op. cit., p. 17.

they only receive rare, incidental mention in his works. Galuppi, Vogler, Avison—most musical people to-day have never heard of them apart from Browning's poetry.

The first published of his great musical poems was *A Toccata of Galuppi's* (*Men and Women*, 1855). Galuppi (1706–85) was a well-known and popular Italian composer in his day, but none of his seventy operas has survived. Browning tells of "Venice and her people, merely born to bloom and droop"—frivolous creatures, with their masks, their mirth and folly, their love-making and kisses, who listened while Galuppi "sat and played Toccatas, stately at the clavichord":

VII

What? Those lesser thirds so plaintive, sixths diminished, sigh on sigh,
Told them something? Those suspensions, those solutions—"Must we die?"
Those commiserating sevenths—"Life might last! We can but try!"

VIII

"Were you happy?"—"Yes!" "And are you still as happy?" "Yes. And you?"
"Then, more kisses!"—"Did *I* stop them when a million seemed so few?"
Hark, the dominant's persistence till it must be answered to!

XI

So, an octave struck the answer. Oh, they praised you, I dare say!
"Brave Galuppi! That was music! Good alike at grave and gay!
I can always leave off talking when I hear a master play!"

A toccata, or touch-piece, in its early days (sixteenth and seventeenth centuries), was a rather showy composition, designed to exhibit the touch and execution of the performer. It was a flowing movement in notes of equal length and of a homophonous character, though Galuppi, with his chords freely used, somewhat elaborated it. Browning in these stanzas refers to the plaintive effect of a minor third. His "diminished sixth" may mean the afflicted minor sixth, but in any case a diminished interval naturally conveys a feeling of sadness; and a "suspension"—holding over a note from one chord to another—produces some form of dissonance which craves a "solution" (i.e., craves to be "resolved"). "Sevenths" are dissonances, and a "commiserating seventh" is probably a minor seventh, which is usually mournful. These dissonances and suspensions, followed by "solutions", correspond to the effect of sorrow and anxiety in real life, relieved by the joy that succeeds them. Then, the love-making starts afresh; but the dominant intervenes and is answered by an octave on the tonic: the toccata is over, and the party of gay revellers breaks up; but—

> in due time, one by one,
> Some with lives that came to nothing, some with deeds as well undone,
> Death stepped tacitly and took them where they never see the sun.

The music had told them they must die; they had gone on dancing and kissing; but death took them in the end. The poet imagines Galuppi's toccata as having a chilling effect—

> In you come with your cold music till I creep through every nerve.

Saul is one of the greatest religious poems in the language. But it is not a story solely of the redemptive power of words inspired by God, or even of poetic words inspired by Him, but of consecrated song—poetry and music combined in His service. It is based on 1 Samuel xvi, 14–23, and tells through David's lips how Saul in his affliction sent for him and how he made his way to the King's tent, spoke to him, tuned his harp and first played the tune to which all the sheep respond and then in turn those that delight the quails, the crickets, and the jerboa (or jumping hare); for all God's creatures are of one family with man; and next he played the reapers' help-tune, and onward he went to the march for the dead man with few faults who is "praised on his journey"; to the glad marriage chant, the great march of human comradeship, and—

> the chorus intoned
> As the Levites go up to the altar in glory enthroned.

And there he paused, for he has accomplished the first part of his purpose. After that, the poet turns to the subjects of which David went on to sing to Saul, and how gradually he restores him to health by dwelling on the joys of living, the goodness of man's life, "God's hand thro' a life-time", the brotherhood of men, friendship, the greatness of kingship, and the "blaze on the head of one creature—King Saul!" By "heart, hand, harp and voice" he leads him on, step by step, to an awakening of the enjoyment of a noble life in the service of mankind, and he ends with a great prophetic cry—

> a Hand like this hand
> Shall throw open the gates of new life to thee! See the Christ stand!

Browning has not, in all this latter part of the poem, dwelt on the actual music which accompanies this inspiring poetry: we are left to imagine it. The whole poem is a magnificent contribution not only to religious literature, but to a subject which has absorbed the attention of doctors—and of mankind generally—for many centuries and particularly in our own day, the influence of music on health.

"Master Hugues of Saxe-Gotha" is a purely fictitious composer, long since dead. In the poem a church organist imagines himself having a "colloquy" with him about the meaning of his "mountainous fugues", and pictures five persons having an argument: it is just like a fugue, with one delivering a phrase, a second answering, a third interposing, a fourth striking in, a fifth thrusting in his nose, and so on. "Is it your moral of life?" asks the organist, with "life's zigzags and dodges, ins and outs". "God's gold" shines, and—

> Truth's golden o'er us although we refuse it—
> Nature, thro' cobwebs we string her.

Hugues' fugue "taxes the finger" and is a "mountain" of tricks. The organist "unstops the full organ" and lets it "blare out the 'mode Palestrina' ". The simple, deeply religious music of Palestrina put an end to the pedantic counterpoint of previous composers, and thereby hangs the true moral of our existence—"the letter killeth, but the spirit giveth life".[1]

Edward Berdoe[2] makes the astonishing statement "Probably Bach's fugues are meant in the poem". They most certainly are not! Bach, of course, lived one-and-a-half centuries after Palestrina, and even in his fugues went further than any of his predecessors in the infinitely varied, but direct, expression of moods, emotions and religious feelings; and Browning himself speaks of "glorious Bach" in Stanza XVI of *Charles Avison.*

The Abbé Vogler (1749–1814) was Court Chaplain at Mannheim and elsewhere and travelled in many countries: he was a minor composer, but evidently a brilliant organist. And Browning in his poem *Abt Vogler* portrays him regretting that his extemporization on the organ could not be a lasting creation. He wishes that—

> the structure brave, the manifold music I build,
> Bidding my organ obey, calling its keys to their work,
> Claiming each slave of the sound,

could be as permanent as a building such as Solomon, who, according to Jewish legend, had sway over angels and demons, might have willed them to erect for the princess he loved. (Music has often been compared to architecture.) Browning's Vogler is conscious of the divine nature of music:

> But here is the finger of God, a flash of the will that can,
> Existent behind all laws, that made them and, lo, they are!
> And I know not if, save in this, such gifts be allowed to man,
> That out of three sounds he frame, not a fourth sound, but a star.
> Consider it well: each tone of our scale in itself is nought;
> It is everywhere in the world—loud, soft, and all is said:
> Give it to me to use! I mix it with two in my thought:
> And there! Ye have heard and seen: consider and bow the head!

[1] 2 Corinthians iii. 6.
[2] *The Browning Cyclopaedia*, fourteenth edition, p. 267.

He can scarcely bear the thought that "the palace of music I reared" is "gone . . . never to be again". But perhaps there will be—

> Many more of the kind
> As good, nay better, perchance: is this your comfort to me?

All this leads him on to trust to God for the immortality of everything that is good:

> no beauty, nor good, nor power
> Whose voice has gone forth, but each survives for the melodist . . ."
> "The high that proved too high, the heroic for earth too hard,
> The passion that left the ground to lose itself in the sky,
> Are music sent up to God by the lover and the bard;
> Enough that he heard it once: we shall hear it by-and-by.

Failure is only a pause in the music, the discords that rush in to make the harmony more prized. Sorrow and doubt obstruct men's path:

> But God has a few of us whom he whispers in the ear;
> The rest may reason and welcome: 'tis we musicians know.

And he ends:—

> I will be patient and proud, and soberly acquiesce.
> Give me the keys. I feel for the common chord again,
> Sliding by semitones, till I sink to the minor—yes,
> And I blunt it into a ninth, and I stand on alien ground,
> Surveying awhile the heights I rolled from into the deep;
> Which, hark, I have dared and done, for my resting-place is found,
> The C major of this life; so, now I will try to sleep.

Charles Avison, an English musician (about 1710–70), was also an organist, and the author of *Essay on Musical Expression*, which aroused controversy by placing the French and Italian schools of music above the German; (he had studied in Italy and was a pupil of Geminiani in England). His compositions are forgotten to-day. Browning's father possessed the manuscript of

Avison's Grand March in C, the music of which Browning quotes at the end of the poem that bears the musician's name (published in 1887). And it was this March—"bold-stepping", yet the unpretentious product of a dead, minor musician—that prompted Browning to compose a poem about music's influence on the mind of man. Here—in contrast to the other musical poems that we have been considering—he refers by name to many of the great composers, including some of his own contemporaries: Brahms, Wagner, Dvořák, Liszt, Handel, Gluck, Haydn, Mozart, and "glorious Bach". He even alludes specifically to the Song to the evening star in *Tannhaüser*—

> "O Thou"—
> Sighed by the soul at eve to Hesperus.

> There is no truer truth obtainable
> By Man than comes of music.

"Soul" rolls as an "unsounded sea" underneath "Mind". But

> Feeling from out the deeps
> Mind arrogates no mastery upon.

> To match and mate
> Feeling with knowledge,

There are—Hates, loves, joys, woes, hopes, fears, that rise and sink

> Ceaselessly.

> How we Feel, hard and fast as what we Know—
> This were the prize and is the puzzle!—which
> Music essays to solve.

"Art" may "arrest Soul's evanescent moods".

> Poetry discerns,
> Painting is 'ware of passion's rise and fall,
> Bursting, subsidence, intermixture—all
> A-seethe within the gulf.

> Outdo
> Both of them, Music! Dredging deeper yet,
> Drag into day—by sound, thy master-net—
> The abysmal bottom-growth . . .

In other poems of Browning music figures incidentally, in varying degrees.

The three *Cavalier Tunes* are songs for solo and chorus, intended to be sung, and subsequently they were set to very stirring music by Stanford.

Up at a Villa—Down in the City is a monologue put in the mouth of "an Italian person of quality" who hankers for life in a city rather than at a villa on a mountain-edge—the city with its fountain, its blessed churchbells, the rattling diligence, its bustle and news and noise—and (twice mentioned) the "bang-whang-whang" of the drum, the "tootle-te-tootle" of the fife. By contrast, in *A Serenade at the Villa,* a lover sings to his lady at her villa on a dark, sultry, summer night—"You heard music; that was I". But—

> What became of all the hopes,
> Words and song and lute as well?

He vowed devoted service to her, as he sang, but she slept on and heeded not his song.

And in *One Way of Love,* too, the lover—

> Strove to suit
> These stubborn fingers to the lute.

Yet—

> She will not hear my music? So!
> Break the string; fold music's wing.

In *The Last Ride Together,* that poem of noble resignation to unrequited love, Browning asks the lover whether the musician, for instance, has attained his object:

> What, man of music, you grown grey
> With notes and nothing else to say,
> Is this your sole praise from a friend,
> "Greatly his opera's strains intend,
> Put in music we know how fashions end!"

In *The Pied Piper of Hamelin,* before we come to the descriptions of the piper and his music, Browning writes of the rats—

shrieking and squeaking
In fifty different sharps and flats.

In *The Flight of the Duchess,* we read of "a fifty-part canon"; of the old witch who—

began a kind of level whine
Such as they used to sing to their viols
When their ditties they go grinding
Up and down with nobody minding;

and of the strange musical sound which the old huntsman heard coming from the young lady's room when the gipsy, changed temporarily into a queen, was bewitching her.

In *The Grammarian's Funeral* the mourners carry the corpse up the mountain for burial "singing together"—"step to a tune, square chests, erect each head".

The Heretic's Tragedy "would seem to be a glimpse from the burning of Jacques du Bourg-Malay (Grand Master of the Knights Templars) at Paris, A.D. 1314; as distorted by the refraction from Flemish brain to brain, during the course of centuries". The Abbot Deodaet and the monks are singing in the choir of their church about this medieval tragedy; there are directions for a "plagal cadence" to be played on the organ, and the instruction—

And wanteth there grace of lute or clavicithern, ye shall say to confirm him who singeth—
We bring John now to be burnt alive.

They seem to gloat over their victim, but the Abbot finally adds—

God help all poor souls lost in the dark.

In *Fra Lippo Lippi* we hear of—

A sweep of lute—strings, laughs, and whifts of song;

and in *Cleon* the poet declares—

I have not chanted verse like Homer, no—
Nor swept string like Terpander, no—nor carved

And painted men like Phidias and his friend:
I am not great as they are, point by point.
But I have entered into sympathy
With these four, running these into one soul,
Who separate, ignored each other's art.

And in *One Word More* ("to E.B.B."), Robert, though so versatile in several arts, is nevertheless modestly speaking to his wife in his own person:

I shall never, in the years remaining,
Paint you pictures, no, nor carve you statues,
Make you music that should all-express me;
So it seems: I stand on my attainment.

He who blows thro' bronze, may breathe thro' silver,
Fitly serenade a slumbrous princess.
He who writes, may write for once as I do.

Youth and Art is the wistful tale of a sculptor and a singer who missed the chance of happiness together.

In *Mr. Sludge, "The Medium"*, we have a reference to Beethoven, and we hear of—

Asaph setting psalms
To crotchet and quaver.

Balaustion's Adventure, too, has occasional references to music:

the strangest, saddest, sweetest song
I, when a girl, heard in Kameiros once,

And who hears music, feels his solitude
Peopled at once—for how count heart-beats plain
Unless a company, with hearts which beat,
Come close to the musician, seen or no?

"For thee, Alkestis Queen!
Many a time those haunters of the Muse
Shall sing thee to the seven-stringed mountain shell,
And glorify in hymns that need no harp, . . ."

We hear of the "spot-skin lynxes" and the lions finding "joy i' the music" of Apollo, and "the speckled-coated fawn" dancing round his lyre.

In *Fifine at the Fair*, Don Juan, strolling with his wife, Elvire, is fascinated by Fifine, the gipsy, with her tambourine. His wife's beauty is in his own sense and soul—he cannot explain the cause, any more than he can account for the effect of music in technical terms—

> And, music: what? that burst of pillared cloud by day
> And pillared fire by night, was product, must we say,
> Of modulating just, by enharmonic change—
> The augmented sixth resolved—from out the straighter range
> Of D sharp minor—leap of disimprisoned thrall—
> Into thy light and life, D major natural?

He answers his wife's scepticism by appealing to music, which can pierce through the False and can—

> let the soul, exempt
> From all that vapoury obstruction, view, instead
> Of glimmer underneath, a glory overhead.

> For this is just the time,
> The place, the mood in you and me, when all things chime.
> Clash forth life's common chord, whence, list how there ascend
> Harmonics far and faint, till our perception end—
> Reverberated notes whence we construct the scale
> Embracing what we know and feel and are!

Don Juan tells how once he turned from speech to music to give utterance to his thoughts, and hit on Schumann's *Carnival* (an anachronism that does not matter) and "played the whole o' the pretty piece", which he describes in vivid terms. And so—"Gone off in company with Music!"—he imagines himself on a pinnacle above St. Mark's Church, Venice, gazing upon a prodigious Fair, in "Carnival-Country". At first, it all seemed revolting, but when he got down among the revellers and found them more human, his feeling gradually gave way to delight. Then he came to realize—

> that what I took of late
> for Venice was the world; its Carnival—the state
> of mankind—

and so he meditates in characteristic Browningesque fashion on "the lesson of a life" . . . Among other things he tells us how the arts and Morality keep shop and adapt themselves to changing times—

> And here's another feud
> Now happily composed: inspect this quartett-score!

> For as some imperial chord subsists,
> Steadily underlies the accidental mists
> Of music springing thence, that run their mazy race
> Around, and sink, absorbed, back to the triad base—
> So, out of that one word, each variant rose and fell
> And left the same "All's change, but permanence as well".
> —Grave note whence—list aloft!—harmonics sound, that mean:
> "Truth inside, and outside, truth also; and between
> Each, falsehood that is change, as truth is permanence . . ."

In *La Saisiaz,* that noble, profound, religious poem evoked by the death of his great music-loving friend, Miss Egerton Smith, Browning wrote—

> Nay, do I forget the open vast where soon or late converged
> Ways though winding?—world-wide heaven-high sea where music slept or surged
> As the angel had ascendant, and Beethoven's Titan mace
> Smote the immense to storm Mozart would by a finger's lifting chase?

(There is also a brief reference to Beethoven near the end of *The Ring and the Book*, Book XII, line 865.)

One of Browning's last poems is *Flute music, with an Accompaniment*. A man hears a "bird-like fluting", and "through the ash-tops" imagines that it must be the expression of all sorts of sweet thoughts and tender emotions; but his lady companion disillusions him: the music comes from a neighbour who "drudges" "deep o'er desk" and is spending a few minutes' leisure with—

> Youth's Complete Instructor
> How to play the Flute,

and his "Tootlings hoarse and husky" have no connection with the ideas fancied by the listener:—

> distance altered
> sharps to flats,

and the "missing bar" was not due to kissing, but to a mistake in the playing. So the man reflects that fancy may be as real as substance—

> Both are facts, so leave me dreaming.

For Browning, music and life go hand in hand. With his profound, penetrating, vigorous mind, how robustly he would have rebutted the twentieth century notion of music expressing nothing but itself !

Lastly, is it fanciful to suggest that this great poet had the musical structure of a "Theme and Variations" subconsciously in his mind when he wrote *The Ring and the Book*?

PART V

CONCLUSION

CHAPTER 21

Serenity

MUSIC CAN EXPRESS all the emotions, in generalized forms. With its help we may worship and pray. It may simply entertain. It can stimulate and encourage. It can also soothe. Indeed, its beneficent effects on health have attracted special attention in our generation.

Serenity, as manifested in music, is so vast a subject that a whole book would be needed to discuss it thoroughly. My object in this chapter is to illustrate the way in which certain composers, either in their general musical mentality or in particular creations of theirs, have evinced a spirit at peace with the world or with God.

Serenity in music is not confined to any one epoch. If a man lives in a peaceful age, he may nevertheless be a rebel against it, and conversely a composer may be capable of such detachment that he can both feel and express tranquillity of spirit though the world around him is wracked and tormented. The works of Palestrina, written for the Roman Catholic ritual in the sixteenth century, were as calm as any music ever created, and the art of William Byrd, whether liturgical or secular, is essentially the outcome of a serene mind. The same can be said, in general, of the vocal and instrumental compositions of the other great English masters of that era—such as Weelkes, Morley, Wilbye, and Gibbons. Yet the Elizabethan age in England could scarcely be called a tranquil one, and this was the time when Marlowe, Webster and Tourneur were producing their grim tragedies on the stage, while Shakespeare, the myriad-minded creator of joyful comedies and even of idyllic romances, passed through a period in which he wrote dramas of tragic intensity and even bitterness of spirit. He may have remained, in his private life, a person of serene detachment from the profound tragedies which he gave to the theatre, but this is quite uncertain. The serenity of the English music in those days is not wholly explained by the fact that the art had not yet developed the resources which were later to enable it to express turbulent emotions and heartrending situations. For even in that epoch Monteverdi, in spite of the limited means at his disposal compared with those of the nineteenth century, was able to convey tragic and pathetic intensity in his works for the stage. He was capable of conveying serenity in his *Vespers* of 1610, but his music-dramas touched a note of perturbation of spirit such as we do not find among his English musical contemporaries.

Music is more independent of the world outside itself than are the other arts, but this does not necessarily mean that composers are so detached in their outlook as to exhibit serenity of spirit in their creations. We should naturally expect to find it in religious music, but even there we meet with exceptions such as those in the *Messe des Morts* and *Te Deum* of Berlioz and the Requiem of Verdi.

In opera the composer is involved in expressing the drama, and the characters and emotions of the persons on the stage, and serene music is not to be expected unless it happens to be appropriate to those. We find it at certain points of Handel's operas, and the tragic grandeur of Gluck's works for the stage does not preclude tranquillity of spirit from being present where the drama evokes it—as, for instance, in the dance of the blessed spirits in *Orfeo*. Among Mozart's operas, real serenity is to be found in the masonic scenes of *The Magic Flute*. Wagner, one feels, was at peace with the world when he depicted in gentle tones the character of Hans Sachs, or painted the heavenly visions of the *Lohengrin* prelude or the devotional piety of the knights of the Grail in *Parsifal*.

Since the sixteenth—or at any rate—seventeenth century (when Purcell was still, for the most part, continuing the serene tradition of his Tudor and Jacobean predecessors), the composers who have shown themselves predominantly serene in their outlook, as evinced in their music, have not been in a majority. Bach, profoundly though he could express the worshipper's grief at the sufferings of Our Lord in His Passion, was majestically serene throughout his life's work. Handel is tranquil in spirit, in many places, but his music sometimes shows a tense dramatic excitement, and his graphic descriptions necessarily precluded serenity on certain occasions; in the main, however, his outlook, so far as his music conveyed it, was serene, though not as consistently so as Bach's. The "demonic" element in Mozart, the rapier thrusts and latent passion in some of his instrumental movements, and the fact that in his operas he naturally sought to express the feelings of the characters, prevented him from being always, or even predominantly, serene as Haydn was. Nevertheless, there is a great deal of serenity in the art of Mozart.

Haydn was one of the most divinely serene of all composers—whether he was conveying the profound religious feeling of the seven last words of the Saviour on the Cross, the happy contentment of so many of his instrumental compositions, the peace of the countryside in *The Seasons*, or the simple faith contained in the music of *The Creation*.

Beethoven is a difficult case to describe. For the most part, he won serenity only as a result of a struggle. We find it sometimes in his early works, before the *sturm und drang* of his maturity had set him upon a new and more deeply emotional track; in the *Pastoral Symphony*, where he voiced real relaxation of spirit; in the violin concerto and particularly in its exalted slow movement; in the Fourth Symphony; and in his third period chiefly through the medium of the string quartet. In the late quartets he often seems to dwell in a world apart, a seer who, in his music, though not in his private human relationships, has taken upon him the mystery of things and attained true tranquillity of soul at last after the stress and tumult of his earlier life. The Ninth Symphony ends in ecstatic, though divine, joy—scarcely serene in character, though serenity is present in the music "where the seraph dwells with God." The *Missa Solennis* contains in the "Benedictus" some of the loveliest serene music ever written, with the violin descending like the dove from Heaven; and the "Dona nobis pacem", after those moments of terror which suggest the distant sound or threat of war, ends in sublime peace and resignation.

Schubert poured forth so rich a profusion of masterpieces that serenity was almost bound to find a place amid the variety of moods which he portrayed. But the essence of his serenity lay in his being the most approachable of all the great composers, so that when he was not striking a note of terror or of power he could be easy-going, gentle, and peaceful, as in so many of his more tender songs, in the Impromptu in A flat for pianoforte, or in the slow movement of the Unfinished Symphony. "Du bist die Ruh' " is one of the most perfectly reposeful pieces of music in existence.

The comfortable and prosperous circumstances of Mendelssohn's life kept him free from the anxiety and turmoil which afflicted Beethoven, Berlioz, and Wagner. They formed the background for the serene, happy music to which his assured and consummate workmanship was wedded. He might sometimes strike a melancholy vein, as in the Andante of the Italian Symphony or the First Allegro of the Trio in D minor, but the melancholy never ran deep, and when we think of the idyllic violin concerto, the light-hearted character of the other movements of the Italian Symphony, the Octet, the tranquillity of the *Hebrides* overture, the fairy atmosphere and the good-humour of the music for *A Midsummer Night's Dream*, and the reflective choruses and arias in *Elijah*, we can truthfully call Mendelssohn one of the most serene-minded of all creative artists, even though this spirit of peace does not in his case go far beneath the surface.

Compared with him, or even with the gentleness of some of Schubert's works, neither Schumann nor Chopin evinces the same degree of serenity. Schumann had too romantic a soul to be capable of being for long at peace with the world, though he had his moments of quiet rapture—"Im wunderschönen monat Mai" or in the delicate sweetness of the slow movement of the pianoforte concerto. Chopin could dream like a poet at the piano, but we do not primarily associate serenity of spirit with his imaginative genius.

The deeply religious caste of mind which characterized César Franck is revealed in a great deal of his music—not only in those works (such as *The Beatitudes*, *Redemption*, the Prelude, Chorale, and Fugue, and the organ works) which in varying degrees were avowedly sacred or even liturgical in character, but in such compositions as the Symphony, the string quartet, the quintet for piano and strings, the Prelude, Aria, and Finale, and the violin and piano sonata, which had no expressed connection with religion. They justify us in describing Franck's musical mentality as, in the main, a serene one. He might depict turbulent emotions and struggles, grief, and even tragedy, but never seems submerged by them. Faith reigns throughout and invariably triumphs in the end. There is a kind of detached majesty about his composition at its best. When he paints Hell (or even Earth) in *The Beatitudes*, he is not at his best, and *The Djinns* and *Le Chasseur Maudit*, for all their vividness, are not characteristic of him.

Brahms, in spite of the vein of Nordic pessimism which appears sometimes in his music—as in the first movement of the D minor piano concerto (until the second subject appears), the introduction and first Allegro of the Symphony in C minor, and certain movements of his chamber music—is, on the whole, a serene composer. The Fourth Symphony may end tragically, but Brahms remains proudly master of the situation. In the *Requiem* there is a lofty elevation of spirit; the composer, one feels, was not bowed down by sorrow, even before he sought—and obtained—consolation in religion. Brahms is nowhere finer than when he is expressing serenity of mind and spirit in his music—in the happy, carefree finale of the B flat piano concerto, in the calm phrases of the Intermezzo in E flat for piano, or the sunny peacefulness of a song like "Am Sonntag".

Among the nineteenth century composers since Beethoven, we shall find none save Fauré comparable to Franck and Brahms in serenity of spirit. Dvořák (often) and Smetana (usually) smile contentedly, and Grieg delights us with the charm of his lighter moments. The Russians are never serene in the true sense of the term. Even Tchaikovsky, commonly supposed to be the most cosmopolitan of them, conveyed no real peace of mind in his music. He charms our senses, and probably soothed his own soul, by the enchantment of his fairy music in *The Sleeping Beauty*, *Swan Lake* and *Casse Noisette;* but his was never truly a serene spirit. He was imbued with a strong vein of melancholy or even morbidity, alternating with triumphant excitement, and the magical world of the ballet, one feels, was a means of escape for him from the brooding sadness and the sensational, brief-lived, outbursts of joy which his more serious instrumental compositions show as musical embodiments of his experiences in his real life. As regards the other Russian masters, no one could single out serenity as a conspicuous feature of any of them; it is indeed scarcely present in their music. Even Berlioz had more of it: the idyllic beauty of *L'Enfance du Christ*, and the classic majesty of parts of *Les Troyens*, are apt to be overlooked by those who concentrate too exclusively on the wilder, more romantic, sides of his genius.

On the other hand, Fauré, who belonged both to the nineteenth and to the early twentieth centuries, wrote many songs that were peaceful in character and his *Requiem* is the most serene setting of this part of the liturgy that ever has been created.

Among his contemporaries, Delius wrote a number of tranquil nature studies for orchestra; yet even these are filled with nostalgia, of a yearning for a lovely past that can never return. His music is scarcely ever really happy. Consciously or unconsciously it marks—together with that of Mahler—the end of an epoch, and however high our hopes for the future, we share these two composers' evident regret at the passing of a world, a culture—call it what you will—which, for all its faults and tragedies, brought us much beauty and many blessings.

Hugo Wolf did for the song, to a large extent, what Wagner did for the opera: but (unlike Wagner) he composed music for the words of others, and he followed the nuances of each poem more closely than any composer of *lieder* before him. Thus he got so much inside the skin of every literary work which he set, that the question whether he was serene-minded is scarcely relevant. If the poetry was tranquil, of course Wolf's music was too; but more often, it was nothing of the kind.

Ernest Bloch, intense, sombre, and monumental, is too imbued with the tragic history of the Jewish people to write music that is truly serene. Manuel de Falla's art is vivid, with a profound charm, and a vein of delightful wit, but except for certain passages in *Nights in the Gardens of Spain*, it is not conspicuous for tranquillity. Sibelius is grand, tragic, austere, profound, and withal sometimes light-hearted and charming; only in the Seventh Symphony does a kind of Olympian calm dominate the scene and bear witness to serenity of mind. Hindemith's *Symphonia Serena* has a certain carefree atmosphere, but is not truly serene in spirit.

And so we find that in recent times serenity in music is more conspicuous in English, and to some extent American, art than in that of other nations. The musical mentality of Samuel Barber and of Roy Harris (as evinced, for instance, in the latter's Third Symphony) shows a fundamental quietness of spirit. Serenity may not be the most marked feature in Elgar's instrumental compositions (except the 'cello concerto and the three works of chamber music written towards the end of his life), but it permeates his great creations of religious devotion—*The Dream of Gerontius*, *The Apostles*, and *The Kingdom*. Vaughan Williams is, perhaps, the most serene composer since Haydn; of course there are exceptions even among his works, for tranquillity is not the dominant quality in the *Sea Symphony* or the *London Symphony*, and the one in F minor is completely devoid of it. The first three movements of the Sixth Symphony are for the most part turbulent in character; even in the quiet epilogue the immortal spirit of man is full of questionings. But works such as the Fantasia on a theme of Tallis, his *Pastoral Symphony*, *Sancta Civitas*, *Dona nobis pacem*, *Job*, and above all the Fifth Symphony and the string quartet in A minor, show an altogether exceptional serenity of soul. It is particularly remarkable that the two last-named compositions should have been written in a world at war—testimonies of the inspired faith of an old man of genius amid the terror and tragedy which surrounded him.

Among the younger generation of English composers, Benjamin Britten, that versatile and prolific artist, was evidently imbued with tranquillity of spirit when he created *A Ceremony of Carols* and the cantata *Rejoice in the Lamb*. And Michael Tippett's *A Child of our Time*, in spite of its passages of deep pathos and fierce indignation, ends on a note of hope and serenity.

Thus even in this age of war and confusion and anxiety the serenity of souls at peace with the world and with God still lives on. We remember Horatio's words as Hamlet dies:

> Good night, sweet prince,
> And flights of angels sing thee to thy rest.

CHAPTER 22

Epilogue

WHITHER DOES ALL this lead us? I have rested in serenity, but I cannot end there. Deryck Cooke[1] has, indeed, shown us how music is, essentially, a language of emotions, and G. Wilson Knight[2] has perceived that great music, like great poetry, extends consciousness, is linked to humanity at every turn, and corresponds to eternity: he cites as instances, Bach, Beethoven, and Wagner. But we need not stop there.

Byrd and Palestrina voiced the divine simplicity of the heart of Christianity in their etherial settings of the Roman Catholic Mass. Handel dramatized the Old Testament, and, in a fortnight, brought Christ to earth again in all the grace and grandeur of *Messiah*. Bach even welcomed death in his cantatas, rose to the heights in the majesty and drama, the terror and pity, of his Passion music and the sublime Christian ritual of the B minor Mass, yet employed counterpoint—one of the most complex of musical devices—for the expression of human moods and feelings. Haydn's consummate art never lost the beauty of childhood; only a man with the heart of a child could have composed the Biblical story of *The Creation* or the wonders of *The Seasons*, late in his life, in the terms in which he did. Mozart is by turns a great poet of laughter, a "perturbed spirit", a master of controlled emotion, a weaver of musical spells that appear simple but are full of innocent subtleties, a genius who harmonized the magic of a fairy story with the world of the spirit.

Yet—

> Pity, like a naked new-born babe
> Striding the blast, or heaven's cherubin, hors'd
> Upon the sightless couriers of the air—

[1] In *The Language of Music*. [2] In *Christ and Nietzsche*.

music never reached that *kind* of utterance until the coming of Beethoven—the Titan who championed man against Fate, sounded the profoundest roots of human feeling, filled the very heavens with divine humour, embraced not only Christianity but all the eternal and sacred verities, and burst even the bounds of his own structures by the range of his prophetic vision.

Schubert was a child of nature, and a poet of nature. His music is sometimes almost incredibly simple, yet at times it strikes depths of terror and tragedy, and expresses either through voice or instruments an endless variety of emotions by means of music which at the same time catches the breath by the sheer loveliness of its sound.

After Beethoven and Schubert, the river of romanticism burst into full flood, which did not abate until the end of the nineteenth century. Berlioz delights, enchants, bewitches, descends into hell, brings hell to earth, and soars into the empyrean. In his *Messe des Mortes* he calls for an enormous orchestra—largely to make it play softly and comfort us with its rich, soothing sounds. In *The Trojans* he alternates glorious love music with the recurring voice of destiny, which gains the ultimate victory by its challenging call to duty. Chopin, the composer of two of the world's greatest sonatas, voiced a man's joys and sorrows, wistfulness and gaiety, despair and courage, through the medium of short pianoforte pieces bearing no titles to explain their message, because none was needed. Wagner, the "mighty-mouthed inventor" of music-dramas, whether using medieval Nuremberg or the world of legend for his purpose, and whether his mythology was Christian or pagan, enthroned love—the love of man and woman, the love of self-expression, the love of self-sacrifice, the love of humanity, the love of friends, the loves of gods or the love of God—as the dominant force in the world—nay, in the universe; for his art, in its vast sweep, is not confined to this earth. Brahms needed no drama to fertilize his music. Without Beethoven's mystic vision or prophetic insight, he probes the depths and range of emotions by means of instruments alone, uplifts us by the Titanic grandeur of some of his creations, and, in others, enchants us by the graciousness of his conceptions; he catches the general spirit, rather than the detail, of a poem in his songs, and it was characteristic of him that in composing a Requiem he turned not to any established ritual or any dramatic framework, but to Biblical and Apocryphal texts of his own choosing, and produced a sublime and perfect whole as a result.

It is too soon to say to what extent the music of the twentieth century is really comparable in universality to that of the great giants of the past. Elgar, in the soaring, searing score of *The Dream of Gerontius,* dared to depict Purgatory and Heaven themselves; he was so golden-hearted a creator that he passed by the vices of Falstaff and idealized him into a genial, cheerful, humorous, boastful, but ultimately pathetic, English knight. Sibelius depicts the grandeur of Nature in the mighty forest storm of *Tapiola,* and the spiritual grandeur of mankind in his symphonies. Nielsen, in his Fifth Symphony, even personifies conflicts of the human soul by different instruments. Bloch reached out to all men through the medium of Jewish ritual in his *Sacred Service.* Holst, both in his music and in his own person, was an unorthodox religious mystic. Vaughan Williams's art was rich in variety, yet based on the two pillars of English folk-song and Christianity. Walton swept us off our feet with the fierce, dramatic, Old Testament intensity of *Belshazzar's Feast,* sounded the depths of spiritual struggle, irony, melancholy, and victory, in his B flat Symphony; and (with Christopher Hassall's help) turned *Troilus and Cressida* into a musical drama of romantic tragedy. Britten transformed Shakespeare's "Dream" into a golden fairy opera, and in the profound inspiration of his *War Requiem* gave utterance to the anguish and the pity of war experienced by the men and women of our time and the Christian prayer for rest, light, and peace eternal.

In these, and other, great instances, the Sound of Life reverberates from generation to generation, voicing the emotions and reflections of men and women, typifying their characters and the drama of their existence, transporting them to fairyland, sweeping them in imagination to hell, carrying them in prayer and vision to Heaven, illuminating the scenes of Nature, glimpsing the mysteries of the Universe.

Index

Aeschylus, 16, 89, 102
Chorephorae, 85–6, 87
Aesthetics and Criticism (Osborne, H.), 42–5
Agate, J., 128
Albeniz, 20
Allgemeine Musikalische Zeitung, 49
All I Could Never Be (Nichols, B.), 65 n. 1
Aristophanes, 102, 103
Birds, 132
Aristotle, 82
Poetics, 24, 90, 102
Arne, Dr., 129
Ashton, F., 72–3, 74
Avison, C., 152, 163, 167, 168

Bach, C. P. E., 38, 45
Bach, J. S., 17, 19, 20, 25, 33, 38, 46, 47, 48, 59, 61, 63, 67, 68, 89, 132, 135, 159, 166, 168, 178, 179, 184
Art of Fugue, 38
Jesu, Joy, 30
Mass in B minor, 17, 184
Passion music, 60, 61, 184
St. Matthew Passion, 30, 59
Second Violin Concerto, 30
Third Orchestral Suite, 29
Wohltemperirte Klavier, 29, 38
J. S. Bach (Schweitzer, A.), 75
Balanchine, 73
Barber, S., 183
Barker, G., 130
Barrett, E., *see* Browning, E. B.
Bartok, 34
Barzun, J. (*Berlioz and the Romantic Century*), 116 n. 1, 143 n. 2
Beaumarchais, 105, 106
Beethoven, 12, 17, 19, 21, 24, 25, 28, 30, 31, 31 n. 5, 44, 45, 46, 47, 48, 49, 52, 63, 65, 66, 67, 80, 89, 116, 154, 155, 159, 160, 171, 173, 179, 180, 181, 184, 185
Concertos, *Fifth Piano*, 38
Fidelio, 62–3, 93, 107, 135, 146, 147, 153
Grosse Fuge, 50, 52
Leonora Overtures, *No. 2*, 54, 64, *No. 3*, 63, 64
Missa Solennis, 17, 30, 179
Quartets, *B flat* (op. 130), 50; *Razoumoffsky No. 1*, 30; *String* (op. 132), 50
Sonatas, *E major*, 30; *Thirty-second*, 159
Symphonies, *Eroica*, 28, 29; *C minor*, 28, 29, 139; *Fourth*, 179; *Fifth*, 44, 45; *Seventh*, 61, 130; *Ninth*, 30, 49–51, 52, 68, 179; *Pastoral*, 54, 139, 179
Trios, *Archduke*, 63; *B flat*, 29, 30
Beethoven and His Nine Symphonies (Grove, G.), 50
Belline, V., 21, 121
Benét, W. R. (*From Robert and Elizabeth*), 156 n. 5
Berdoe, E., 166 n. 2
Berg, A., 34
Wozzeck, 34, 46, 99, 100
Berlioz, 15, 20, 26, 27, 46, 47, 80, 88, 107, 108, 129, 143, 180; *Memoirs*, 116 n. 2, 117–26; Shakespeare's influence on, 116–26, 133
Béatrice et Bénédict, 108, 125–6
Enfance du Christ, 18, 182
Fantastic Symphony, 139
Harold in Italy, 32, 139
King Lear, 119, 120
Lélio, 119, 120, 121
Messe des Morts, 18, 178, 185
Roméo et Juliette, 32, 120–3, 142, 143
Te Deum, 18
Trojans, 94–5, 116, 125, 143, 178, 182, 185
Tempest, 119
Berlioz and the Romantic Century (Barzun, J.), 116 n. 1, 143 n. 2
Bizet, 20, 83
Carmen, 95–6
Symphony in C, 73
Blagden, I., 158
Blake, W., 74
Bloch, E., 21, 67, 182
Sacred Service, 47, 186
Blom, E., 52, 59
Boito, 112, 114, 135, 136
Borodin, 21
Botticelli, 16
Boulez, 36
Bradley, A. C. (*Oxford Lectures on Poetry*), 136 n. 1
Brahms, 12, 17, 20, 23, 25, 51–6, 67, 168, 181, 185, 186
Academic Festival Overture, 54
Alto Rhapsody, 55
Clarinet Trio (op. 114), 53
Four Serious Songs, 56
German Requiem, 18, 25, 55, 181, 186
Intermezzo (op. 117, no. 1), 32
lieder, 22, 55–6
Nänie, 55
Neue Liebeslieder-Walzer, 55, 56
Quartets, 53

Quintets, 53
Second Piano Concerto, 32
Sonatas, 53
Symphonies, 53; *First,* 31, 53; *Fourth,* 30, 73, 181
Tragic Overture, 19, 54
Variations on St. Antony Chorale, 29, 54
Bridell-Fox, Mrs., 152
Britten, B., 20, 35
Albert Herring, 114
Ceremony of Carols, 47, 183
Midsummer Night's Dream, 114–15, 186
Peter Grimes, 46, 99, 100, 114
Prince of the Pagodas, 74
Rape of Lucretia, 83
Rejoice in the Lamb, 47, 183
Spring Symphony, 47
Brown, M. J. E. (*Schubert, A Critical Biography*), 30 n. 5
Browning, E. B., 153, 155, 156, 157, 158, 160, 161, 171
Letters to Her Sister, 157 n. 8
Browning, R., 12, 16, 151–74
Abt Vogler, 166–7
Balaustion's Adventure, 171
Cavalier Tunes, 169
Charles Avison, 166, 168
Cleon, 170, 171
Fifine at the Fair, 172
Flight of the Duchess, 170
Flute Music, 173
Fra Lippo Lippi, 170
Grammarian's Funeral, 170
Heretic's Tragedy, 170
La Saisias, 173
Last Ride Together, 169
Master Hughues of Saxe-Gotha, 165–6
Mr. Sludge, "The Medium", 171
One Word More, 171
Pied Piper of Hamelin, 169, 170
Pippa Passes, 152
Ring and the Book, 173, 174
Saul, 164-5
Serenade at the Villa, 169
Toccata of Galuppi's, 163–4
Up at a Villa—Down in the City, 169
Youth and Art, 171
Browning Cyclopaedia (Berdoe, E.), 166 n. 2
Bruckner, 21
Bückner, 99
Bunyan, 83
Busoni, 45, 65, 83
Byrd, W., 20, 25, 37, 38, 46, 177, 184

Caccini, G., 76, 102
Calderon (*El Purgatorio de San Patricio*), 79
Calvocoressi, M. D. (*Modest Mussorgsky*), 41 n. 7
Cardus, N. (*Ten Composers*), 113 n. 4
Chaucer, 100
Cherubini, 21
Ching, J., 132
Chopin, 21, 22, 24, 25, 37, 67, 72, 107, 180, 184
Études, 24, 32
Nocturne in G, 24
Piano Concerto in F minor, 32
Preludes, 24
Christ and Nietsche (Knight, G. W.), 84 n. 2
Cimarosa, D., 154
Colles, H. C., 52
Constable, 47
Cooke, D. V. (*Language of Music, The*), 26 n. 1, 184 n. 1
Corelli, A., 154
Corot, 47
Cortot, 65
Couperin le Grand, 20
Cranko, J., 73, 74
Crown of Life, The (Knight, G. W.), 137
Crozier, E., 114
Curtis, G. W., 156
Czerny, 49

Dante, 16, 20, 82, 89
Divina Commedia, 82, 103
Dearest Isa (McAleer, E. C., ed.), 158 n. 14
Debussy, 20, 33, 35, 60, 67
Delius, 20, 67, 78, 182
Paris, 72, 73
Song of the High Hills, 46
Dent, E. J. (*Mozart's Operas*), 37 n. 2
Divine Quest in Music, The (Mendl, R. W. S.), 17 n. 1, 19 n. 2, 23 n. 4, 28 n. 3, 39 n. 3
Dohnányi, 73
Donizetti, 21
Donne, J., 24, 152
Dowland, J., 20, 155
Dufay, G., 20
Dunstable, J., 20
Duparc, 60
Dvořák, 20, 168, 181

Edward Elgar (McVeagh, D.), 40 n. 5
Egk, W. (*Irische Legende*), 84
Einstein, Alfred (*Greatness in Music*), 15
Elgar, 20, 23, 25, 40, 67, 139
Apostles, 47, 183

'Cello Concerto, 32, 183
Dream of Gerontius, 47, 55, 68, 183, 186
Enigma Variations, 32
Falstaff, 40
Kingdom, The, 47, 183
Violin Concerto, 38
Ella, J., 159
Elwes, G., 65
Essays in Musical Analysis (Tovey, D. F.), 28 n. 4, 40 n. 4, 45 n. 11, 120 n. 6
Euripides, 89, 90, 102
Electra, 85, 86, 89

Falla, M. de, 20, 74, 182
Three-Cornered Hat, 73, 74
Faure, G. U., 20, 60, 181, 182
Feeling and Form (Langer, S. K.), 26 n. 1, 43, 76 n. 1
Finzi, G., 129
Flagstadt, K., 65
Flower, E., 152
Foakes, R. A., 137
Fokine, 72, 74
Fornier, E., 126
Franck, C., 20, 72, 180–1
Symphony, 53, 139, 180
From Robert and Elizabeth (Benét, W. R.), 156 n. 5

Galuppi, B., 163–4
Gebler (*Thamos, König in Aegypten*), 79
Gibbons, O., 20, 177
Gilbert, W. S., 102, 111–12
Giotto, 16
Glazunov, 72
Gluck, 21, 25, 32, 103, 141, 168
Alceste, 78, 92, 93, 168
Armide, 141
Don Juan, 78
Iphigenia in Auris, 92
Iphigenia in Tauris, 92
Orfeo ed Eurydice, 63, 77–8, 84, 91, 92, 141, 178
Paris and Helen, 141
Glyndebourne, 72, 78
Goethe, 16, 55, 60, 89, 119
Goodwin, N., 88
Gounod, 83, 142
Granados, E., 21
Greatness in Music (Einstein, Alfred), 15
Grieg, 21, 181
Griffin, W. H. and Minchin, H. C. (*Life of Robert Browning*), 152 n. 2, 153, 156 nn. 6, 7, 158 n. 12, 162 n. 20
Grove, G. (*Beethoven and His Nine Symphonies*), 50; *Dictionary*, 41 n. 6
Gui, V., 64

Hadow, W. H. (*Oxford History of Music*), 37 n. 1
Hallé, C., 157, 159, 160
Handel, 17, 20, 25, 28, 30, 38, 68, 92, 93, 154, 155, 168, 178, 179
Largo, 30
Messiah, 55, 61, 184
Ptolemy, 30
Hanslick, E., 110
Harris, R., 183
Hassall, C., 100, 186
Haydn, 17, 18, 24, 25, 30, 30 n. 5, 38, 52, 129, 139, 168, 179, 183
Creation, 18, 179, 184
Seasons, 18, 179, 184
Seven Last Words, 18
String Quartet (op. 77, No. 1), 31
symphonies, 24, 31, 44
Heine, 60
Hesse, M., 65
Hiller, F. von, 158
Hindemith, 35, 83, 183
Hofmansthal, H. von, 83, 85, 88, 99
Holderlin, 55
Holst, G., 20, 67, 186
Hymn of Jesus, 47
Savitri, 83
Homer, 16, 89
Hood, T. L. (*Letters of Robert Browning*), 161 n. 18, 162 n. 20
Horowitz, V., 65
Humperdinck, 112, 113

Illustrated London News, 118

Jaňăcek, 21, 100
Jeune, C. le, 154, 155
Joachim, J., 159, 160, 162
Johannes Brahms (Specht, R.), 52
Josquin des Prés, 20

Keats, 24
Klemperer, O., 66
Knight, G. W. (*Christ and Nietsche*), 184 n. 2; *Crown of Life*, 137; *Shakespearean Tempest*, 151
Kodály, 47
Krehbiel, H. E., 51 n. 2
Kreisler, 66

Lachmann, H., 88

La Fontaine, 118
Lamond, F. A., 65
Langer, S. K. (*Feeling and Form*), 26 n. 1, 43, 76 n. 1; *Philosophy in a New Key*, 43, 76
Language of Music, The (Cooke, D. V.), 26 n. 1, 184 n. 1
Lassus, O., 20, 38
Lawes, H., 155
Letters of Robert Browning (Hood, T. L.), 161 n. 18, 162 n. 20
Lewis, R., 65
Life and Letters of Robert Browning (Orr, S.), 151 n. 1, 157 nn. 10, 11, 160 nn. 15, 16, 161 nn. 17, 19
Life of Ludwig van Beethoven (*Thayer*), 51 n. 2
Life of Robert Browning (Griffin, W. H. and Minchin, H. C.), 151 n. 2, 153, 156 nn. 6, 7, 158 n. 12, 162 n. 20
Liszt, 15, 22, 51, 54, 55, 67, 159, 168
Livermore, A. L., 79
Lully, 21, 54, 77

McAleer, E. C., ed. (*Dearest Isa*), 158 n. 14
McVeagh, D. (*Edward Elgar*), 40 n. 5
Mahler, G., 21, 24, 66, 182
Fourth Symphony, 68
Massenet, 83
Massine, 73, 74
Matthews, D., 65, 132
Melba, N., 65
Memoirs of Hector Berlioz (Holmes, R. and E.), 116 n. 2, 117–27
Mendelssohn, 21, 25, 41, 46, 129, 180
Bee's Wedding, 129
Elijah, 180
Hebrides Overture, 180
Italian Symphony, 180
Midsummer Night's Dream music, 128–33, 180
Octet, 129, 180
Scotch Symphony, 129
Trio in D minor, 180
Violin concerto, 129, 180
Mendl, R. W. S. (*Divine Quest in Music*), 17 n. 1, 19 n. 2, 23 n. 4, 28 n. 3, 39 n. 3; *Soul of Music*, 7, 16, 19 n. 2, 21, 23 n. 4, 27 n. 2, 35 n. 6, 39 n. 3
Menuhin, Y., 66
Messager, A., 112
Messaien, 35, 36
Michelangelo, 16, 89
Milton, 16, 151, 156
Minchin, H. C. and Griffin, W. H. (*Life of Robert Browning*), 152 n. 2, 153, 156 nn. 6, 7, 158 n. 12, 162 n. 20
Modest Mussorgsky (Calvocoressi, M. D.), 41 n. 7
Molière, 103, 118
Monaldi, 137
Monteverdi, 20, 178
Orfeo, 77, 91, 141
Vespers, 178
Moonlight at the Globe (Watkins, R.), 128, 128 n. 1
Morley, T., 20, 177
Mozart, 17, 18, 25, 30, 30 n. 5, 31, 37, 38, 52, 67, 93, 107, 110, 113, 141, 168, 179, 184
Cosi fan tutte, 104, 105–6
Don Giovanni, 62, 63, 76, 78, 79, 92, 103–4
Entführung aus dem Serail, 104–5, 141
Figaro, 18, 31, 84, 104, 105, 106
Idomeneo, 18, 78, 92, 103
Magic Flute, 18, 79–80, 104, 107, 142, 178
Mass in C minor, 18, 37
operas, 37, 92, 141–2
String Quartet in D minor, 31
symphonies, 139; *Linz*, 18; *G minor*, 29; *Prague*, 18
Mozart's Operas (Dent, E. J.), 37 n. 2
Musical Times, The, 40
Music and Letters, 7, 79
Music of Liszt (Searle, H.), 15
Mussorgsky, 20
Boris Godounov, 41, 83, 96–7, 139
Kovantschina, 83

Nash, H., 65
Nervac, G., 119
Newman, E., 49, 50, 75, 89, 116 n. 2; *Opera Nights*, 88, 113 n. 3; *Wagner Nights*, 81–2
Nichols, B. (*All I Could Never Be*), 65 n. 1
Nielsen, C. A., 21, 23, 186
Nietzsche, 81
Nikisch, A., 66

Observer, The, 59, 83
Offenbach, 102, 110
Olivier, L., 132
Opera Nights (Newman, E.), 88, 113n. 3
Orr, S. (*Life and Letters of Robert Browning*), 151 n. 1, 157 nn. 10, 11, 160 nn. 15, 16, 161 nn. 17, 19
Osborne, H. (*Aesthetics and Criticism*), 42–5
Oxford History of Music (Hadow, W. H., ed.), 37 n. 1, 52
Oxford Lectures on Poetry (Bradley, A. C.), 136 n. 1

Pachmann, V., 65
Paderewski, 65, 66
Paganini, 66
Paisiello, 160
Palestrina, 20, 38, 166, 177, 184
Parry, C. H. H., 132
Pears, P., 114, 115
Pergolese, G. B., 156
Peri, J., 76, 102
Petrassi, G., 68
Pheidias, 16
Philosophy in a New Key (Langer, S. K.), 43, 76
Poetics (Aristotle), 24, 90, 102
Ponte, da, 105, 106
Promenade Concerts, 67–8
Puccini, 21
  Boheme, 65, 76
  Tosca, 98
Purcell, 20, 143, 178
Purgatorio de San Patricio, El (Calderon), 79

Rameau, J. P., 20, 77
Raphael, 16
Ravel, 21, 68
Rawsthorne, A., 132
Regan, A., 160
Relfe, J., 152
Rembrandt, 16, 89
Richter, 66
Rimsky-Korsakov, 21, 46, 72, 97
  Coq d'Or, 113
  Scheherazade, 74
Rossini, 20, 110, 154, 155
  Barbieri di Siviglia, 106, 107
  Cenerentola, 107
Rubens, 16
Rubinstein, A., 65, 159, 160
Ruskin, 157
Ruysdael, 47

Saint-Saëns, 83
Samuel, H., 132
Sargent, M., 61
Scarlatti, A., 20
Scarlatti, D., 20, 38, 46, 132
Schiller, 49, 55
Schnabel, A., 65
Schönberg, 33–4, 35, 36; Dodecaphonic scale, 33–6, 38
Schubert, 17, 18, 21, 25, 30, 47, 59, 129, 179–80, 185
  Impromptu in A flat, 180
  lieder, 23, 55, 65, 67, 160
  Quintet in C (op. 163), 31
  symphonies, 68, 180
Schubert, A Critical Biography (Brown, M. J. E.), 30 n. 5
Schumann, C., 162
Schumann, R. A., 21, 67, 72, 180
  Carnaval, 172–3
  lieder, 23, 55
Schütz, H., 21
Schweitzer, A., 59
  J. S. Bach, 75–6
Searle, H. (*Music of Liszt*), 15
Shakespeare, 12, 16, 18, 24, 42, 60, 63, 89, 103, 129, 140, 151, 156, 177; cuts to plays, 60–4; Falstaff in, 40, 136; influence on Berlioz, 116–27, 133; Verdi and, 133–7
  Coriolanus, 116
  Hamlet, 82, 116, 117, 118, 119, 121, 124, 134, 184
  Henry IV, 40, 112, 116, 136, 138; *V, VI*, 138; *VIII*, 137–40
  King Lear, 116, 134
  Macbeth, 96, 116, 127, 133–4
  Merchant of Venice, 116, 124, 125, 143
  Merry Wives of Windsor, 112, 136
  Midsummer Night's Dream, 114, 115, 116, 128–32, 186
  Much Ado about Nothing, 108, 116, 125, 126 n. 15
  Othello, 116, 134, 135, 136
  Romeo and Juliet, 116, 117, 118–19, 120, 121–3, 142
  Tempest, 116, 121
  Troilus and Cressida, 101, 116
Shakespearean Tempest, The (Knight, G. W.), 151
Sharp, C., 130
Shelley, 24, 155
Shostakovitch, 35
Sibelius, 21, 23, 34, 67
  Tapiola, 47, 140, 186
  Tempest music, 129, 140
  Seventh Symphony, 23, 24, 47, 139, 140, 182
Smetana, 21, 108–9, 181
Smithson, H., 117, 118, 119–20, 124
Solomon (pianist), 65
Sonnleithner, J., 49
Sophocles, 16, 89, 102
  Electra, 85, 86
Soul of Music, The (Mendl, R. W. S.), 7, 16, 21, 19 n. 2, 23 n. 4, 27 n. 2, 35 n. 6, 39 n. 3
Specht, R. (*Johannes Brahms*), 52
Stanford, C. V., 161, 169
Stern, I., 66
Stockhausen, 36
Strauss, Johann II, 25, 110–11
Strauss, R., 21, 22–3, 84
  Alpine Symphony, 22
  Ariadne auf Naxos, 83
  Don Juan, 23, 47
  Don Quixote, 22, 23, 46

Electra, 23, 85, 86–9, 99
Heldenleben, 22
Macbeth, 23
Metamorphosen, 23
Rosenkavalier, 22, 113
Salome, 46, 98, 99
Sinfonia Domestica, 22
Till Eulenspiegel, 22, 23, 46
Tod und Verklärung, 22, 88
Stravinsky, 35, 36
Firebird, 73, 74
Petruchka, 46, 73, 74
Sullivan, A., 20, 24, 102, 110, 111–12
Sunday Times, The, 49, 88, 89
Sutermeister, 142

Tallis, 20
Tchaikovsky, 20, 25, 32, 181–2
Casse Noisette, 181
Romeo and Juliet, 142
Sleeping Beauty, 73, 74, 181
Swan Lake, 73, 74, 181
symphonies, 139
Ten Composers (Cardus, N.), 113 n. 4
Thamos, König in Aegypten (Gebler), 79
Thayer, A. W. (*Life of Ludwig van Beethoven*), 51 n. 2
Theodorakis, M., 74
Times, The, 23 n. 5, 62
Times Literary Supplement, 15
Tippett, M., 83, 84
Child of Our Time, 183
Midsummer Marriage, 76, 83, 84
Titian, 16
Tobin, J., 61
Toscanini, 61, 66, 130
Tovey, D. F., 50, 120; *Essays in Musical Analysis*, 28 n. 4, 40 n. 4, 45 n. 11, 120 n. 6
Tree, H. B., 60, 61
Treitschke, G. F., 64
Tureck, R., 132

Vaughan Williams, R., 20, 67, 129, 183, 186
Dona Nobis Pacem, 47, 183
Job, 47, 73, 74, 183
Mass in G minor, 47
Pilgrim's Progress, 83
Sancta Civitas, 47, 183
Serenade to Music, 125
String Quartet in A minor, 183
symphonies, 47, 183
Tallis Fantasia, 183
Velasquez, 16
Verdi, 20, 40, 41, 49, 65, 80, 113; Shakespeare and, 113–17
Aïda, 97–8
Falstaff, 31, 112, 114, 133, 134, 136–7, 144
Four Sacred Pieces, 31, 134
Macbeth, 133, 134, 137
Otello, 31, 98, 114, 133–7, 143, 144, 146
Requiem, 31, 68, 178
Rigoletto, 76, 133
Traviata, 133
Trovatore, 173
Vergil, 16, 116, 124
Vinci, Leonardo da, 16
Vittoria, T. L. de, 20, 38
Vogler, G. J. ("Abt"), 163, 166

Wagner, R., 18, 31, 32, 37, 40, 47, 51, 59–60, 65, 66, 67, 71, 88, 91, 113, 135, 160, 168, 180, 182, 184
Fliegende Holländer, 80, 93
Götterdämmerung, 68 n. 1, 93, 94, 138, 145
Lohengrin, 80, 81, 93, 178
Meistersinger, 19, 31, 80, 84, 109–10, 144
Parsifal, 19, 31, 33, 80, 81–2, 93, 178
Rheingold, 93, 138
Ring des Nibelungen, 19, 31, 76, 80, 81, 84, 93, 138, 144, 145
Siegfried, 93, 138, 145
Tannhäuser, 80, 93, 168
Tristan und Isolde, 18, 31, 33, 81, 93, 94, 115, 144, 145–6
Walküre, 31, 68, 93, 138, 144–5
Wagner, W., 64
Wagner Nights (Newman, E.), 81–2
Walter, B., 66
Walton, W., 20, 35
Belshazzar's Feast, 186
Symphony, 186
Troilus and Cressida, 100–1, 186
Watkins, R., 132, *Moonlight at the Globe*, 128, 128 n. 1
Weber, C., 21, 80, 107
Euranthe, 107, 142
Freischütz, 80, 107, 142
Oberon, 107, 142
Webern, A. von, 35, 36
Weelkes, T., 20, 177
Weinberger, J., 113, 114
Wilbye, J., 20, 177
Wilde, O., 88
Williams, R. Vaughan, *see* Vaughan Williams
Wolf, H., 18, 19, 21, 59, 182
Grenzen der Menscheit, 24
lieder, 23, 25, 55, 182
Prometheus, 25
Wordsworth, 16, 24, 45, 47